Emotional Maturity

In Everyday Life

Kosjenka Muk

Table of Contents

Disclaimer:

Parts of this book might trigger strong emotions and unpleasant memories. If you feel overwhelmed or unable to cope, please stop reading and remind yourself that those are just memories of the past. If you feel unstable, please consult a helping professional.

Warning: you might feel a temptation to interpret ideas from this book in simplified or even extreme ways. Do not do it. Consider the complexities of each situation you want to deal with.

This book represents the opinions and experience of the author. Avoid using this book against your own experience and common sense. The author takes no responsibility for any unwanted consequences that might be attributed to careless use of this book. The reader accepts full responsibility for his or her decisions and behavior.

Preface

Many people invest huge effort into avoiding effort. Promises of magical, overnight solutions are often very attractive. When those promises fail, as they will, people seek short-term relief and escape from reality. This damages their emotional maturity, awareness of genuine emotions and true identity.

Although physical and material aspects of life are important and unavoidable, I primarily see the true potential for happiness in having quality, fulfilling relationships with oneself and others, as well as developing our creativity and other potentials.

This cannot be achieved overnight – it requires long-term self-observation, uncompromising honesty to oneself, investing effort into changing our automatic reactions and commitment to exploring our inner world. The rewards are many: supportive intimacy with ourselves, warm and fulfilling relationships with others and courage to take risks and to experience life fully... to name only a few.

Our society is emotionally immature and this is generally perceived as normal and acceptable. Children growing up in such an environment will adjust to it by creating beliefs and emotional patterns that enable them to survive - and years later, these might be difficult to change.

Oversimplifying is a defense mechanism most commonly used as a refuge of immaturity. You can recognize it in nationalism (masked as "patriotism"), all kinds of prejudice and narrow-mindedness - and in instant-solutions to life and relationship problems. I want this book to be an antithesis of oversimplifying - to take into consideration the complexity of human lives and emotions, and to emphasize the importance of finding balance instead of following exaggerated ideas.

When I use expressions such as "childish" and "immature emotions", some people might interpret this as criticism. This is not my intention – I simply want to define and describe a specific type of emotional reactions. I define "immature" emotions as those that have been suppressed during childhood, when we were small and powerless. At that time, we did not have the resources to deal with them and to learn to express them in a mature manner. Those emotions are triggered and often burst out and take over in situations that remind us of past moments in which we experienced something similar.

This is unavoidable – everyone carries such suppressed emotions within themselves. If you recognize yourself in some of the situations described in this book, it only shows that you are normal, not that something is wrong with you. From time to time, I recognize myself in many of the examples described throughout the book. I wrote many chapters while I was exploring my own feelings.

I do not want to encourage blaming anyone (people often blame parents or society for their emotional problems). It is crucial to become aware of our individual responsibilities in seeking personal transformation and to discover our innate potentials.

Practically everybody has emotional problems – this is a consequence of living in emotionally unhealthy surroundings. We do not create emotional problems by accident; we use them as defense mechanisms. In other words, we reject parts of ourselves and our emotions, since it is the only way we know how to deal with unhealthy circumstances.

According to psychoanalytical theory, a mentally ill person is the one who is unable to build strong enough defense mechanisms against pain. Defense mechanisms can often be unhealthy and have unpleasant consequences (like avoidance, denial, projections...) but are better than losing our minds.

Our limiting and toxic beliefs are also defense mechanisms. We create them as children in attempt to understand and assimilate unexpected and painful (from the child's point of view) events. They defend us from even greater loss – loss of family bonds and safety, perhaps even loss of physical and mental health which might follow after the shock caused by the conflict between inner and outer reality.

Children younger than five (especially babies and toddlers) are still perceived by some people as not much more than cute animals, rather than sensitive and complex human beings. If adults believe that small children cannot suffer the consequences of an experience, wrongly assuming they are unable to perceive, understand and remember what is going on, they will likely be insensitive of their behavior in front of the children. It begins with the separation of a baby from her mother in a hospital, followed by family conflicts, worsened by parental criticism or over-protection and so on.

The next reason for inconsiderate behavior to children can come from the expectation that children are able to understand, remember and predict things in the same manner as an adult. This is not true. Compared to animals, we are all immature at birth, with underdeveloped brains not yet capable of basic survival. If human babies were born at the same level of maturity as animals, their heads would be too big to pass through their mother's vagina. The brain of a human child needs a lot of time to grow and mature, and some adults, who have not been educated about it, can have difficulties understanding it.

Until recently, it was believed that newborn babies could not feel all human emotions. In the 19th century (according to J. M. Masson and S. McCarthy), it was believed that newborns and small children were unable to feel physical pain. It was quite normal at that time to perform painful surgery on children without anesthetics, ignoring their screams of pain. It is possible that such lack of empathy among those who promoted this idea, was a result of the way they were treated by their early family.

On the contrary, especially in earliest stages of life – as evidenced by results of many modern scientists who researched the prenatal period – children are very sensitive of their surroundings, including subtle nonverbal gestures and emotional atmosphere around them. Some scientists now claim that small children can be up to seven times more sensitive to non-verbal communication than adults can. The foundation of our personality is thus created within those first experiences and becomes a kind of filter for all subsequent experiences. Most people later consider this to be a coincidence or genetic heritage.

Many people live empty and dry lives, deprived of feelings of adventure and passion. They do jobs they dislike, with a quality of life barely better than a few centuries ago. For years, even decades, they stay in relationships that lack intimacy and respect, and believe that it is normal that the quality of their lives is just above plain survival. I often think that in terms of meaningful careers, relationships and quality of life, human kind has not advanced much further from Middle Ages behavior.

Can you imagine living with enthusiasm, passion, serenity and strength? With full awareness about your own worth? Imagine that you naturally create healthy and mature relationships, that it is normal for you to express yourself wisely and feel comfortable around other people. How would that feel? How would your life change?

Even if we are so used to our patterns of feelings and thoughts that it might seem impossible or very difficult to change, it can be done. If you want to succeed in personal development, you need to be willing to face even the most immature parts of yourself. You have to take the responsibility for changing your life. The reward is a true and permanent improvement that reaches the very core of your personality. Only committed effort can create visible, permanent results in your relationships and life.

Deep honesty to yourself is the first step on the journey towards your happiness and health.

Self-Esteem as a Foundation for Emotional Maturity

I begin this book with the topic of self-esteem, since I believe that true emotional maturity is not possible without a basic experience of self as worthy of love. People who do not love themselves, in my opinion, cannot truly love or appreciate other people. They might consciously try, but fear, anger and shame accumulated under the surface will often motivate them to act defensively or criticize others, just to be able to bear with their own negative self-images.

Few things are "black" or "white"; there are only "shades of gray" between the two extremes. In one moment, we feel appreciated, and in the next, we can feel humiliated and insignificant. Some parts of our personality are healthy and fully aware of reality, while other parts might be hidden in unresolved, long ago suppressed complexes.

What exactly is self-esteem?

In a society that is on a low level of emotional development, in which most people rarely have the chance to experience what it like is to feel truly good about themselves, it is useful to clearly define self-esteem.

What I want to talk about is far more complex and larger than self-esteem defined just as the way somebody acts or the way somebody perceives herself.

I want to talk about the feeling of deep inner fulfillment, pure pleasure of existence, experience that is beyond love for oneself. I want to talk about the experience of being the source of love itself. At this point, the expression "love for oneself" becomes an unnecessary rationalization. Self-esteem might not adequately describe this inner state, but it can be used to describe the behavioral habits that result from this state.

Even when we talk about behavior itself, our society is not familiar with self-esteem and so it is interpreted in many different ways.

In ancient times, our ancestors were brought up to be obedient to rulers and priests. To achieve that, it was necessary to force people to give up their natural desire for freedom and a better life, to make them think less of themselves, to suppress their inherent, authentic feelings and aspirations. For many centuries, since the earliest ages, people were brought up in fear, guilt and shame not only for the slightest mistakes in behavior, but simply for harboring 'incorrect" emotions (e.g. "anger is a deadly sin"). Feelings of love for self, experiencing self as a valuable human being – would automatically mean disregarding and rejecting imposed fear and guilt, and therefore were not allowed.

For people to believe that their deepest feelings were bad, they had to be convinced that they were sinful and unworthy by nature. When children brought up in that kind of environment grew up and had children of their own, their offspring's immature behavior thus provoked deep feelings of insecurity, guilt and shame. Often it was easier for such parents to call the children "bad" or "selfish" than to admit their own feelings of fear, guilt and shame, which had been suppressed for decades. This is how guilt and fear are often passed on to next generations.

In such a way, a society of false politeness and doubtful morality was created, a society in which "being good" meant to neglect yourself and your own needs, "being polite" meant not to disagree or stick out, not even to say something good about yourself, and "consideration for others" often meant damaging yourself.

A basic law of physics says that energy cannot be destroyed; it is only possible to change its form. A similar law applies to emotions.

Suppressed emotions linger within us and strive to rise to surface and give us their messages. If we do not allow ourselves to face them in a constructive way, unconsciously we start to look for relief in other ways– often destructive ones. Gossip, hypocrisy, depression, envy and malice provided pressure relief for many generations. Sooner or later, self-control is not enough to sustain the pressure of accumulated emotions and we switch to another extreme.

This is occurring in our civilization right now. Accumulated destruction rises through countless images of violence and immature behavior on television. Younger generations, which on one side were brought up on tradition and on the other side with such immature models that send the message that destruction is OK, turn to the other extreme –

open selfishness, arrogance and aggression. Some people call this self-esteem, which is one reason for confusion about the term.

Many people have never experienced true self-esteem and have only a whimsical image of how is it expressed. It is easy then to believe in false portraits of self-esteem, in an often fake, superficial feeling of power that destruction might give. Once you have your own inner experience of self-esteem, no longer do you need outer models for self-orientation.

If you ever felt arrogance, contempt or aggression – and from time to time this happens to everyone - you have probably noticed that it is not a truly pleasant feeling. Instead of appreciation for oneself, those attitudes are based on fear, defensiveness and attempts to avoid perceived dangers, including trying to suppress unpleasant feelings. On the other hand, when we truly appreciate ourselves, we are spontaneously more willing and able to see the positive qualities of other people. Therefore, true acceptance of oneself is naturally related to the acceptance of others. On some level, we are aware that the human essence is the same for all of us, and whatever we find within ourselves, we spontaneously search for within others as well.

Behavior that appears to be confident, but without consideration and respect for others, is not self-esteem but only hides subconscious negative self-images. You have probably experienced that those attributes you know you possess, you do not feel you have to prove or actively point out to others. The need to show off, to prove yourself, implies that you do not quite trust your qualities or who you are.

Each and every one of us has some negative beliefs about ourselves, and consequently we feel the need to prove the opposite to ourselves and to others. This can be a very strong, compulsive need that is hard to moderate or, sometimes, even to be aware of. Much of what we do or yearn for is motivated by that need. How would it look like if, instead of needing to prove ourselves, we really felt good about ourselves? How much energy and time in all areas of our lives would become available for much more useful purposes?

A young woman I will call Irene came to me with a desire to build her self-confidence and to feel that she deserves to be loved. Although gentle, sophisticated and intelligent, she felt insecure and was afraid to express herself.

Irene had a habit of continuously analyzing her behavior, especially when she wanted to express some of her feelings. Then she would imagine all the unpleasant conclusions that someone might make about her behavior and would use those thoughts to criticize herself. She used to imagine all sorts of ways in which someone might misinterpret her words or intentions, usually in the worst possible scenario. This was particularly a problem in situations when other people's reactions to her were not entirely positive. At that point, she would start to believe that she truly had the bad intentions she imagined someone might attribute to her, instead of holding on to the awareness of her own truth. Sometimes just imagining criticism would cause her to feel like an ashamed little girl.

While researching those infantile emotions, Irene felt that, when she was a small child, she was constantly under observation and her behavior and words were always criticized. She felt that her parents very often interpreted her behavior in the worst possible manner, telling her that she was selfish and that her intentions were bad, while her good qualities and good intentions were rarely noticed. That is quite a common attitude – most of us are much more likely to focus on discomfort rather than pleasure; probably a heritage from our evolution through which our ancestors had to be constantly alert to any sign of danger.

As a child of three or four, Irene instinctively trusted her parents, but could not understand their real reasons for criticizing her. As a result, she started to believe many of those criticisms, in spite of her feelings whispering that something was wrong. As she grew up, not only it became normal for her to treat herself in the same way as she was treated before; she was also attracted to relationships in which she experienced similar behavior, since she learned at a very young age to associate love with criticism.

As a part of the healing process, I asked her to imagine what it would feel like if her parents had noticed and appreciated the best in her and interpreted her behavior in a positive way. During this exercise, she experienced a perspective that had been almost unimaginable to her: to naturally accept herself and to feel love for herself, to feel that she is a good person, and to spontaneously recognize distorted perceptions that many people have in everyday situations.

True self-esteem and respect for others

In external behavior, self-esteem is expressed as respect for our feelings, our needs and demands as well as respect for other people; this means, amongst other things, to see others as powerful and capable of doing the same. There is no fear of condemnation (which is actually fear of self-criticism!). The need to neglect ourselves to take care of others disappears because we know that they can take care of themselves and, not less relevantly, that it is their right to do so.

The anger and resistance that we might feel in situations when others try to express their discomfort with our behavior, or when they warn us that we have violated their personal boundaries, is a defense mechanism which conceals deep unconscious beliefs that we don't deserve to stand up for ourselves. Those beliefs are usually created at a very young age. Still, in some ways, a child will feel that such a belief is unnatural and will resist it. At a young age, however, he does not know how to deal with such inner conflict and confusion. Thus, a feeling of inadequacy is often covered up with a compulsive need to defend our self-image by underestimating or even humiliating other people and their feelings and needs.

This need to avoid feeling inadequate is partly fueled by a biological urge for power and competition. The evolution that shaped our genes includes a conflict between cooperation and empathy, on one hand, and domination and power, on the other. Yet, I find that family upbringing shapes our biological heritage, not the other way around. A child who is taught self-esteem as well as healthy boundaries, can find constructive ways to distinguish himself and express his power and abilities.

A healthy and happy child, one who has not yet learned to feel ashamed of herself, will spontaneously express her wishes and feelings without even thinking to conceal them – at least until she is taught otherwise. A healthy child primarily focuses on herself, and naturally, although not consciously and rationally, expects others to do the same. If parents neglect themselves to please her, this is just as confusing and damaging as if they neglect her in order to please themselves.

To focus on self – doesn't it sound selfish? By default, it is labeled as selfishness. Often it's easier to call this selfishness in others, than to take care of ourselves, to confront someone, to say "no" or to stand up for ourselves. **Respect for other people is an essential part of true self-esteem.** We respect other people's personal boundaries when we avoid hurting them intentionally or endangering their freedom — but also by being aware of their power and responsibility to stand up for themselves and protect their boundaries. In other words, to warn us if, unintentionally, we do something that makes them feel uncomfortable.

When I talk about focusing on yourself, I mean that only you can know what you want and need. We cannot expect anyone else to be accurate in predicting our desires and needs. In the same way, we cannot know what other people want or feel. Since each one of us has a different personality and history, often we will be wrong even when we are convinced that we know what another person is feeling or thinking.

I am NOT advising ignoring others and avoiding doing anything nice for them, as some people with black and white perception might say. It is nice to help people around us feel better! Sometimes we might want to give up something that is not so important to us, or to do something that makes the other feel good, even if it takes effort. It all comes down to balance. It is essential to be aware of your important values and needs while being considerate to others. Everything else can be negotiated and a healthy person will not expect to have it all her way.

You won't see a healthy and happy child, who feels good about himself, trying anxiously to predict and guess what people around him think or want ("Have I said something wrong?", "Have I done something wrong?", "Might people think that I am selfish?"), but you will meet a lot of unhappy, anxious people (and children) who do exactly that. For a healthy child it is normal to say "no" if he doesn't want something, that other people also say "no" and set their boundaries — and then to negotiate.

Nevertheless, very often people close to a child are unable to set boundaries or sincerely express themselves, so they either blame or try to manipulate others. This is how children learn to feel guilty if they are spontaneous and sincere; and they also learn to blame and manipulate others. People who believe that they will be punished if they are sincere or ask for what they want, will expect others to "read their minds" and predict their needs, which is an awful burden for everyone and an important cause of disputes in our society.

To focus on yourself includes taking full responsibility for yourself and recognizing the responsibility of others to do the same. If everyone was free to express what they feel and want, this would sets us free of immense guilt and endless, often unexpressed, expectations.

It does not mean that others are less important to us. A person who truly feels good about herself does not have the need or desire to hurt or undervalue anyone. Actually, the opposite is true: the more we understand and appreciate ourselves, the easier we can understand others. It is normal to have a general, healthy idea about what it means to intentionally violate the freedom and personal space of other people, and therefore to avoid doing that, since we know how it feels. In an ideal situation, everybody expresses his or her wishes, feelings or disapproval without blame, fear or guilt. In this way, it would be much easier to listen to and appreciate other people's points of view.

Such ideal situations of course are rare, so we need to take into account other people's personal histories, behavioral patterns, fears, guilt and suppressed emotions – just as our own. We will often be in situations when other people cannot consider our feelings and limitations. That makes the work on self-esteem, as well as life itself, diverse, interesting and full of opportunities to learn and to question ourselves from different points of view and in all kinds of circumstances.

Need for love

The need to feel loved and appreciated is one of the strongest drives of human behavior. Yearning for approval is in the core of almost everything that we communicate or avoid to communicate, in most things that we try to achieve and manifest; it is the key to most of our emotional reactions, especially the unpleasant ones.

Do you feel anger or sadness when there is something you want from others but somehow fail to get? Other people's attention is deeply important to us, from "What will the neighbors say?" to extreme exhibitionism. Many people subject their whole lives to it: from people who are never able to express their true wishes due to fear of being rejected, to those who spend all of their lives chasing money to buy status symbols in hope that others would admire them.

When we are children, our families are the only source through which we can evaluate our behavior and ourselves. Inexperienced about the world we are born into, we see our reflections in other people's reactions. As young children, we could not know that other people reacted not only to us, but also to many other things going on in their minds (including subconscious minds).

We reach for power when, unconsciously, we feel that whatever we do, we still do not receive love. This is a painful and terrifying conclusion that is reached at a very young age. Later it turns into a need to control our environment. Another reason for focusing on power is the compensation mechanism: if I can't get what I truly want – to feel worthy through the experience of love – I will reach for something less worthy, but still rewarding, that feels like approval. Therefore, we start to seek dominance.

A search for external love can never replace loving ourselves from within. When we achieve success in outer world, deep down we may feel that it has no true value. We may feel that people's approval is based on an illusion, rather than perceiving who we really are. However, if we never learned how it feels to be loved and appreciated, we do not know any better and stubbornly keep following the old path – the path on which so many people spend their whole lives, repeating strategies that do not work. Even if they achieve external success, they will soon forget it and compulsively reach for more – more fame, more power, more money - yet no external experience of success ever reaches their *inner child* so that they can feel that there is finally enough.

As adults, we can be at least partly aware of what is going on, but old beliefs from childhood are still deeply suppressed and will shape our consciousness and our lives. This can be changed, but not overnight. For many people, the experience of feeling unloved and unappreciated for who they were, became a foundation on which they built their personality, and it takes time and continuous effort to change it.

Miranda, a woman in her forties, was an unwanted child whose parents were pressured into getting married when the mother was pregnant, not because they were in love. During her childhood, her parents kept making this clear to her both verbally and non-verbally. Her father was often away from home, immersed in his job, avoiding his unwanted family.

Many children who grow up in such an environment dissociate,

14

becoming rational people who avoid feelings at all costs. With Miranda, it was different, since her family allowed her to express her feelings to some degree. She grew up to become a person who felt intense emotions, but at the same time, she was influenced by a strong experience of rejection.

She spent most of her life moving from relationship to relationship, always searching for love and attention and imposing huge demands on her partners. Sometimes she would purposely confront them with emotional outbursts, to check if they would accept and support her anyway. Naturally, it was impossible to create a balanced adult relationship through such childish behavior.

Deep toxic beliefs like "I am not worthy", "Something is wrong with me", "I cannot be myself", "I do not deserve happiness", "Life doesn't make sense" etc. – these painful impressions may be deeply suppressed but are the root of most long-term problems. They were created long before we learned words and rational thinking, so they are sometimes difficult to put in words. **Since they were not created rationally, we cannot dissolve them rationally.** A way to heal them, a way to talk to those parts of us is through deep emotional experience. Healing requires changing the emotional components of our early memories, as well as creating new, supportive experiences.

True love for ourselves will fulfill us in ways that no external love could ever do. Even if people love us, but we lack love for ourselves, we will never be able to fully accept it, appreciate it and feel that their love is justified.

You might not be aware of how much better it would feel to love yourself. Imagining such a feeling compared to real experience is like imagining a trip compared to actual traveling.

Our true nature cannot be destroyed; even the most painful experiences in our childhoods can only hinder and hide it until we are strong and mature enough to deal with them. We can discover and experience our true nature again.

Yet it takes time to come to that point. You will have to let your emotions come to the surface, resolve numerous layers of limiting beliefs and practice a healthier state of mind. From my own experience, I know that it is possible. Maybe you will spend some time procrastinating and making mistakes – just as I did – but if you never begin the process and keep striving in spite of mistakes, you cannot expect anything to change.

The feeling of being loved within can heal many small and even bigger hurts and resentments. You will no longer need approval and external confirmations of your worth, so you will feel much more freedom to be yourself. You will better empathize with others and recognize their pain, while still seeing them as strong adults. On the other hand, if somebody hurts you directly or tries to put you down, you will be more capable to stand up for yourself or to turn away and leave.

You will be more willing to make changes and take risks that are too frightening for many people. From this healthy state of mind, you cannot easily accept bad conditions any more: poor working circumstances, harassment at work, dull, hopeless relationships. Without too many words and theories, you know that you are capable and deserving of creating something better. Spontaneously, you move towards your goals and it gets easier and easier, since you are open to learn your lessons – and loving yourself is one of the most important lessons in life.

Points to ponder:

How do you normally perceive yourself? Can you imagine how you would feel if your self-image would dramatically improve?

In which ways do you try to gain attention, recognition and power?

Do you respect other people's boundaries and their freedom? If sometimes this is difficult to do, why is it? What are you afraid of?

What are the working conditions, or relationships, that you know you would not tolerate (for example, insults, physical abuse, poor salary...)? How does that feel? How do you see yourself in those moments, when you know you can do better?

What are the circumstances that you are not happy about, but you tolerate them anyway? How do you feel about yourself then? What beliefs make you accept those circumstances? How do you see life and the world from that perspective?

Practice:

Observe yourself in situations when you feel very happy and good about yourself. How do you see other people then? How do you treat them?

Explore the situations when you feel bad, embarrassed or uncomfortable. How do you see other people then? Is it easier or more difficult to hurt them in this state of mind, compared to when you feel good?

Observe your feelings in situations when you want to feel power over somebody, or to hurt or humiliate someone. What is behind that need? What feelings are you trying to avoid in that way?

What is Emotional Maturity?

Compare your behavior with the behavior of an emotionally healthy child (although with the average upbringing most children lose their emotional health very soon): how much of that curiosity do you still have? ... that playfulness... mobility... openness... energy... trust... joy of life...? Can you imagine bringing those qualities back into your life? These are our true qualities, which cannot be destroyed; we can cut them off and bury them under limiting beliefs, during unpleasant experiences, but we can access and live them again.

Emotions are "voices of our soul", parts of us that are closest to our inner core, to our primordial, spontaneous and intuitive being. Whenever there is a conflict between rational thinking and emotions – if the emotions are healthy – my experience leads me to believe that emotions will usually contain information that is more relevant.

Emotions offer information of how the deepest, truest parts of ourselves experience what is going on around us. Emotions are messengers from the huge reservoir of the unconscious rather than limited rational knowledge. Whenever somebody violates our personal boundaries and integrity, even in a subtle way, our emotions will warn us much faster than our logic. They can warn us about the danger of manipulation, exploitation or other kinds of hurt. Unfortunately, we are trained to censor them much more than we are even aware of. Often we will notice this in others, but not so much in ourselves.

Subliminal, emotional parts of us will register much more information about other people's personalities and intentions, than our conscious minds can interpret. They can register every detail in others' nonverbal signals and offer the inner knowledge that we call intuition.

Facing our emotions

Since emotions are parts of our core being, we cannot ignore them without consequences. In my opinion, too many religious and New Age approaches suggest that people reject, ignore, conquer or "rise above" emotions, resulting in deep inner conflicts that can lead to even more suppression, control and fear of self-awareness, less tolerance and less consideration for other people's point of view.

Even people who are truly committed to personal development, sometimes have difficulty facing unpleasant emotions. Most unhealthy emotions are deeply connected to a toxic self-image. Becoming aware of them can be unpleasant – but less unpleasant than people often fear. Fear of our own emotions is usually acquired in childhood, too, if we felt overwhelmed by them or were punished for them.

When we block unpleasant emotions, we also block pleasant ones, since they are all intertwined. To small, dependent children, immature behavior of people around them can be so frightening that they try to absorb the shock by creating limiting beliefs and suppressing their feelings. The reason it is so hard to resolve those feelings and become aware of them is that infantile parts of us, once dissociated and suppressed from consciousness, never had the chance to mature. They stay on a childish level of perception even when we grow up. Even now, they are still just as afraid of difficult emotions, as when they were originally created.

Healthy and unhealthy emotions

How can we distinguish healthy from unhealthy emotions? Here are some guidelines:

Healthy (adult) emotions:

- The intensity of emotions is appropriate to the situation (in everyday situations, it's usually mild discomfort, like a warning)

- Healthy emotions motivate us, give us energy for appropriate action, for example defending our boundaries and integrity

- We usually have no problem expressing them, as those parts of us were able to mature because they could be recognized and expressed within our families. (We might feel problems and tension, though, if our adult emotions are mixed with unhealthy feelings and guilt. This is most common, since many people learn at an early age to feel guilty if they express their feelings sincerely.)

- There is no tension and discomfort left once the situation is resolved

- There is no black or white attitude, we perceive both sides of the story

- We do not feel humiliated or bad about ourselves, nor do we feel a need to humiliate or hurt others.

<u>Unhealthy (childish) emotions:</u>

- are either overly intense or suppressed

- They are followed by an inner conflict, usually between guilt (*maybe it is my fault*) and shame (*I acted stupidly*) on one side, and anger (*they have no right to treat me like that, I should tell them what they deserve!*) on the other, accompanied by unpleasant bodily sensations. This conflict can persist long after the unpleasant situation is over. Even if you are objectively right, such emotions can show you that there is a part of you that either is frightened or feels guilty. Some childish emotions can feel good temporarily (arrogance, spite...) but the inner conflict remains.

- These inner conflicts sap your energy and, if prolonged, result in stress and tiredness

- You feel that you are (primarily) right, and the other person (primarily) wrong (sometimes the other way around, although that is more common with children or extremely abused people)

- You feel uncomfortable and doubtful about yourself, which may motivate you to criticize and find even more faults in other people.

Sometimes, details in other people's behavior trigger very strong emotions, so strong that we are easily convinced that they are justified, even if everyone, including our common sense, tells us that our reactions are too intense. This can often happen in intimate relationships, since they arouse our deepest emotions. In those moments, it is difficult to stop thinking about the other person's behavior and take responsibility for our emotions – but at those very moments, this is most important and brings most benefits.

Physical discomfort is a common signal that something is suppressed – a feeling of pressure, a soft cramp, pain or burning sensation in the body. For example, if we feel hurt or threatened, usually some immature part of us will surface, for example a part that believes that we somehow deserved the hurt, even if we are rationally aware of reality. To suppress those uneasy feelings and defend themselves, most people use counter-attack or start blaming others. The more intense your fear and guilt are, the bigger is the need to criticize not only the behavior, but also personalities of others.

As we can experience every day, this process happens almost unconsciously and is rarely questioned. During such moments, physical discomfort continues and intensifies, sending warnings that we are missing something. If we fear confronting those unpleasant emotions, it seems much easier to continue the same behaviors (although they do not bring results), rather than to focus inside and face our pain.

Accepting responsibility

I would define emotional maturity as accepting responsibility for our feelings, our experiences, our behavior and circumstances in our lives.

One of the easiest ways to avoid unpleasant emotions, and one of the hardest to unlearn, is passing responsibility to others by pointing out mistakes in their behavior. Even if you are right, when you notice that you keep thinking about the actions or faults of others, imagining what you would like to say to that person, while at the same time feeling uncomfortable sensations in your body, you can be sure that you are avoiding something (for example, fear, guilt or a feeling of inadequacy). It is very easy to get caught up in this process, especially if you realize that the other person is passing responsibility to you too. Then both of you can be caught in a direct or indirect "ping pong" game – a game called "Who started it first" - with both players feeling more and more attacked and therefore attacking back.

In the long term, you can create more and more similar feelings, until you finally decide to take full responsibility to resolve them. You can be certain that you have resolved the cause of a problem when a challenging situation no longer triggers unhealthy emotional reactions. For example, healthy anger will come up if there is a necessity to react, but in healthy anger, there is no need to hurt others or humiliate them, more an urge to set boundaries. Afterwards, if your reaction was constructive and appropriate, there are no lingering unpleasant feelings.

In my opinion, a foundation of successful self-development is an ongoing awareness of our feelings. In this way, we can recognize issues that we have to confront, build true intimacy with ourselves, honesty to ourselves, which leads to self-esteem.

Sometimes unpleasant situations can be so frightening that we would rather do anything else rather than confront them. Yet this very fear of confrontation is a major cause of discomfort. If we can overcome it and allow ourselves to fully accept our feelings, we will usually experience that they are much less unpleasant and frightening than we thought.

When we are afraid or embarrassed to express our emotions, we give ourselves messages that our needs are not important. On the other hand, it is wise not to send others the same messages by acting as if only our feelings matter. Be aware that there are many ways to express the same emotion. The words that first come to your mind might not be the most mature of all.

Forced positivity

Many authors emphasize the power of positive thinking, gratitude and forgiveness. By itself, this makes a lot of sense. However, if we try to use these ideas to avoid our limiting beliefs about ourselves – for example when we try to love ourselves despite feeling inadequate, or when we tell ourselves that we can do anything but do not trust our abilities – if we observe our feelings, we may notice that to every positive thought, our unconscious will respond with opposite, unpleasant thoughts or feelings.

This can be noticed especially when we try to forgive someone rationally (by willpower). Forced forgiveness is an attempt to destroy or suppress infantile anger, which might have been present for decades in our subconscious. True forgiveness comes spontaneously and without effort, as a sort of "side effect", when we resolve our childish emotions, just as true positive thinking comes as a result of resolving beliefs that supported fear and shame.

Many books do not mention such resistance, perhaps considering it unimportant or advising readers to eliminate *negative* thoughts by constantly repeating *positive* ones. When I started working on my personal development, I spent years trying to practice such ideas. I did achieve some improvements – especially if the goals were easy – but after some time I felt that this practice created a constant inner struggle. I had neither the willpower nor the energy to continue. I achieved much faster results using methods like Soulwork Systemic Coaching, which acknowledge emotions and deal with their roots – relationship entanglements, emotional traumas and other experiences that contribute to toxic beliefs.

The more we suppress our unpleasant feelings, the less we can let the wonderful and pleasant feelings flow. Just like we cannot separate one part of our bodies from the rest (except if we REALLY want to suffer), we also cannot isolate one emotion from the others; they are intertwined.

While working on self-improvement, many people experience ups and downs and crises. Soon after achieving wonderful, uplifting states of mind, unpleasant, previously suppressed emotions may surface. In this kind of work, it is necessary to be prepared to accept and work with emotions that might have been suppressed even for decades. They might overwhelm you unexpectedly, discourage you for a while, even frighten you sometimes. However, with time, as you learn to truly love yourself, those unpleasant periods become shorter and milder, until you reach a basically positive state of mind. From thereafter, self-improvement can be a pleasure and not "work" at all. With a free flow of feelings, there will be space for inspiring and surprisingly intense emotional experiences.

Points to ponder:

Do you follow belief systems that encourage certain emotions and motivate you to avoid others? What happens to the rejected emotions? What could be the consequences of such an approach in the long term?

Do other followers of the same belief systems appear to be truly calm and positive, or only superficially? Has the quality of their relationships with themselves and with important people (especially their families) increased or decreased since they adopted these beliefs?

How do those people behave in emotionally challenging situations and crises? How do they treat people who do not fit their criteria or who challenge their beliefs?

Practice:

Have you ignored your feelings and later regretted it? Why did you decide to ignore them? What kind of similar situations can you expect in future? How will you choose which emotional urges to follow, and which not to?

Notice if physical discomfort follows if you ignore your emotions. Consider what you might be avoiding or denying.

Practice discriminating between healthy and unhealthy emotions. During the course of a few weeks, try to notice every emotion as it happens, and then determine: is its quality and intensity appropriate to the situation? Can you express it easily? Does it pass quickly and leave a relatively pleasant "afterglow", or does it leave a lingering feeling of uneasiness? What are the different physical sensations between healthy and unhealthy emotions?

Why People Fail to Achieve Results

Many times, I have heard people wonder, and I have often asked myself the same question: Even after years or decades dedicated to personal development, why do so many people fail to achieve significant and visible results?

Maybe you know people that take pride in their years of self-improvement, yet their behavior shows rigidity and stagnation. What causes this?

Workshops on self-improvement have been popular for several decades. Perhaps you can remember expecting a lot from a method and participating with great enthusiasm in workshops, only to notice that after a few months your enthusiasm weakened, your expectations diminished and after a few years you concluded that you did not truly achieve any benefit! Did you then start searching for some new and more powerful system that would give you the results you wanted? I have been through a few similar cycles myself.

After a while, even the most motivated people usually relax and dedicate about half an hour a day to personal improvement work, whilst the rest of the time they act and think in the same way as before. No matter how often I emphasize the importance of ongoing efforts, from time to time I catch myself doing the same thing.

In my opinion, trying to control our thoughts is definitely not enough. Quite a few authors claim that if we simply ignore "negative" thoughts and emotions, they will be transformed through positive energy. My experience tells me that even if this were true, it's an endlessly slow path compared to acknowledging your "negative" emotions and working with them directly.

Being honest to yourself

It is important to consciously face our emotions, because most of us suppress our unpleasant feelings even when it is not our intention. Trying to avoid unpleasant emotions, which is so strongly promoted in many New Age approaches, leads to even more suppression and requires huge effort. In addition, suppression often causes inner conflict, guilt and feelings of failure, since unpleasant emotions are powerful energies that search for ways to communicate to us.

The motivation behind unpleasant emotions is basically positive: we created them as "healthy reactions to unhealthy circumstances" (R. D. Laing). Those emotions and beliefs continue to try to serve us in ways that reflect the circumstances in which they were created.

One of my favorite principles is: be honest to yourself. By this, I do not mean self-criticism, but rather an attitude of deep acceptance and a willingness to face your most difficult emotions. The best way to motivate yourself is to love yourself and focus on long-term happiness instead of forced perfectionism.

It is difficult to consciously recognize which parts of us hinder us most from moving forward. Those emotional blocks we are aware of, may not be the crucial ones. If we are aware of them, it means we do not perceive them as dangerous enough to suppress. To discover the most important blocks, the resolution of which would bring the biggest benefits, we must carefully observe our emotions and behavior, as well as the circumstances we attract (or are attracted to).

We can learn to recognize emotions that appear in our consciousness just for a moment, before being almost instantly suppressed. When you become skilled in observing your body and feelings, you will notice some light, strange unpleasant sensations starting to appear, which you almost automatically suppress by distracting yourself. It is a subtle process and it takes practice to learn to observe it.

The motivation for such fast suppression of emerging emotions is usually to avoid strong discomfort, or the awareness of their apparent irrationality or destructiveness. This is accompanied by a sense of guilt or fear about this destructiveness. The suppression mechanism is usually created in childhood and sustained until we stop noticing it altogether.

I suspect that the key reason we are not honest enough with ourselves is primarily a deeply suppressed self-hatred. It prevents us from recognizing our destructive emotions without guilt and/or the devastation of our fragile self-images. In such circumstances, we may try to be "superhuman" and prove our value through painfully exaggerated demands on ourselves, not allowing ourselves to be real human beings. This commonly leads to dogmatism and intolerance in our behavior.

No method of self-improvement is likely to motivate us to be willing to look into the most hidden parts of ourselves. It is not enough to learn a technique; the intention and determination to be honest and to truly change have to be conscious and include our whole being. If there is inadequate motivation; if the technique is used to achieve superficial goals, or to avoid responsibility for our lives, or as an escape from real life and true emotions... then the result will be stagnation at best.

It is crucial to explore your most destructive urges, which threaten to damage your image of who we want to be. Pay special attention to those emotions that are, in real situations, the most difficult to bear (such as shame, guilt, humiliation, envy...). Also, notice situations in which you try to distract yourself from your feelings through smoking, food, watching TV, books, computers and many other creative ways. Notice which life situations you automatically avoid because you are afraid of them. Explore which emotions you expect might surface if you faced those situations.

The irrational, almost fully suppressed and, at first glance, unexplainable negative emotions usually appear just for a moment. We then suppress them even before we can become aware of them. However, those issues are often the most important ones to work with. Most people focus on emotions they are aware of and are ready to accept – which are the ones we are less afraid of, so it is easier to let them become conscious. When we explore our most "negative" impulses, we will also find our most limiting beliefs. Once we resolve them, we can enjoy huge relief and change.

When you become sufficiently aware, many emotions that you did not suspect existed may come to the surface. At first, becoming aware of those taboo emotions may cause you to doubt yourself and question whether you really are who you thought you were. Nonetheless, when you let go of your criteria and expectations, you may come to know a deeper level of truth. Your armor of negativity, no matter how horrible it might seem, hides your true identity and deep, subtle, exceptionally pleasant feelings.

Practice:

Practice observing your emotions and writing them down as often as possible. What emotions do you spontaneously and automatically try to suppress even before you truly feel them? What emotions make you angry with yourself?

To work with these issues, you can use the process "Exploring Emotions" in the appendix of this book.

Quantum Leap in Consciousness

A quote attributed to Einstein says that we cannot resolve a problem at the same level of thinking we used when creating it. This is especially true regarding emotional problems and life situations.

Often we find ourselves within a disappointing circle of emotions and thoughts focused on trying to change external situations or other people. Even after making a rational decision, we will probably delay it or suffer inner conflict, which will likely sabotage action.

Within such inner conflicts, each of your urges, emotions and thoughts contain some truth and some healthy and justifiable desires, yet they cannot encompass wider perspectives. Before we finally resolve our limiting beliefs and emotions, each of these urges will alternately appear accurate and realistic. After we heal our limitations and, particularly important, after we integrate our lost and forgotten qualities, we can comprehend a Zen saying: *the opposite of a truth is also a truth*. We can look at problematic situations with deeper understanding and insight, and, more importantly, without emotional limitations. At that moment solutions can become obvious, just as when we observe people wrestling with their own problems.

For example, imagine being unsatisfied with the quality of your intimate relationship. Maybe there is an ongoing battle inside you between anger, love, defiance, fear... You might have thoughts like: 'but he is better than many others.... better to be with him than to be alone... but I do not feel valued or recognized as much as I desire... but sometimes he is very caring... what if I wouldn't be able to find another relationship... but still I desire much more than this relationship can give me...'

Trying to change another person or external environment, or making a rational decision, will not make sense in such a situation. Even if we succeed (usually only temporarily), the root of the problem remains unresolved, emotions remain unhealed, lost parts of us remain inaccessible, and we will quickly create, or will be attracted to similar situations or similar feelings, until we finally decide to look within and start resolving the cause of the problem.

Split personality

Traumatic experiences and toxic relationships can fragment our personalities. We can replace parts of our identity with limiting beliefs, perhaps losing access to qualities such as self-esteem. We may suppress other parts that remain immature (inappropriate feelings), whilst others create compensatory masks (e.g. aggressiveness, victim playing). Sometimes even positive qualities may be used in this way, such as an overt intellectualism, sexuality or humor.

After we resolve our limiting beliefs, we can integrate, for example, lost self-esteem, optimism or joy. Only then it may become obvious, depending upon the situation, that we were, for example, reacting strongly to details that we could have resolved through honest, calm conversation. Perhaps we neglected ourselves out of fear that we did not deserve what we wanted, or that we could not find anything better. Maybe we understood it rationally a while ago, but similarly - as when one tries to guide a friend towards a rational and positive resolution to her problem - the same emotions and fears would reemerge that kept us back.

Attempting to choose between the rational and emotional, between one emotion and another, can be maddening. The conflict continues until we reach a degree of integration from which we can feel and act at a new level of maturity and health. That is truly a quantum leap in consciousness.

It is easy to neglect our own contribution to the problem, to follow immature emotions, which in such moments seem very realistic, and put off their resolution "for later". Procrastinating like that, we can spend years or decades in unnecessary frustration, instead of utilizing that time improving ourselves and creating a happy and healthy life. When I think about the improvement I achieved in the past 10 to 15 years, compared to my starting position, I am impressed – and sometimes I wonder where I would have been now if I had not spent years in procrastination and inadequate efforts.

Practice:

When you find it difficult to make a decision, or when you do not know how to solve a problem (especially a relationship problem), feel and observe the emotions and thoughts that appear. What stops you from acting in the way you feel is right and healthy?

Explore which motivation is at the root of every emotion and urge you have. What do those parts of you want? Maybe security, feeling of importance, power, love, freedom...

For example, maybe one part of you does not want to leave your partner because it wants and hopes to receive love. Yet, another part of you wants to leave this partner and look for a new one, because it wants more respect. Explore what feelings or beliefs stop you from believing that you can have both at the same time.

Use the process "Exploring Emotions" in the appendix of this book.

Intimacy With Our Own Feelings

Every method of personal development that requires clients' cooperation and emotional involvement, assumes that the clients will have adequate awareness of their emotions for the work to be successful. It is unlikely to find books or workshops that include a different possibility. In practice, however, this ideal is not always achievable.

About 20 percent of people I work with (most people who come to me are self-motivated, so I suspect that the percentage is higher in general population) are very disconnected from their emotions and do not normally explore them deeper than just at the most superficial level. This is manifested in several ways:

-they cannot separate personal feelings from the outer situation and examine them independently (i.e. explore the other possible causes)

- they cannot describe deeper and subtler levels of emotions besides the most obvious or most intense ones

- they cannot recognize the beliefs at the root of those emotions.

Generally, such people are unable to notice and thoroughly explore different levels of their emotions, so they often limit themselves to rational analysis. Rational analysis is great for objective, measurable external events; our emotional lives do not follow the same rules.

I find this to be the key obstacle to successful coaching or therapy. Quite often, the clients are aware of this, but in spite of all their effort, they might feel that their emotional awareness persistently slips away, to the point that they start to doubt their capability to feel their emotions.

Since emotions are more instinctive than thoughts, I believe that a person without emotions does not exist (except maybe for those with rare neurological issues). To say that someone cannot feel is like saying that she cannot think or breathe. Emotions are the basis of our self-awareness and an important source of information about our environment and ourselves. Just as we cannot stop thinking for an extended time, it is even less possible not to feel. If we neglect this natural ability and avoid being aware, it can become weaker or less available, but with practice we can make it grow stronger again.

Not only do we all continually experience emotions, but also each of us, at any moment, could access rich, complex emotional states. Some emotions last longer, are more subtle and feel like the foundation of our personality, while emotions on other levels are more intense but shorter lasting. Some emotions are extremely gentle and subtle, they appear for just a moment, yet can open doors to unusual thoughts and perceptions, to creativity and intuition.

Intimacy with our emotions opens us to a deep sense of identity - a strong inner core, which is not accessible through our rational minds only. People who are not in touch with it, might live their whole lives in an almost robotic way, putting bureaucracy and trivial everyday details above their own and others' humanity; or they might feel chronically "scattered" and lost.

Lack of contact with feelings is also at the root of immature behavior. From time to time, you certainly find yourself thinking of someone: "I don't understand how he can't see what he is doing!". People might be aware of their strong superficial emotions, e.g. anger, but be unable to distinguish between healthy and immature, inappropriate anger, or not able to realize that their anger might be hiding some other emotions (like fear, shame etc.).

Dissociation can also cause lack of empathy for other people. Furthermore, such people might even find it difficult to feel compassion for themselves, to be honest with themselves, and to consequently develop healthy self-esteem. We all suppress our emotions to some degree, so it is not so much a question of whether this problem exists or not, but rather to what extent it is present.

The origins of emotional dissociation are often hidden behind decades of avoidance and suppression. This usually starts when a child's emotions are humiliated, punished or ignored by parents and teachers. Other causes include traumas and relationship disappointments that were too painful and intense for a child to deal with. There are no short-term solutions for this. To people who face this problem, I usually advise at least a few months of practicing becoming more aware of their emotions, before we can continue with sessions.

Sometimes, through Soulwork Systemic Coaching, we can explore what was the cause of dissociation – but, as Soulwork is based on emotional experience, this must be explored on an emotional level too. Without the client having some awareness of what he feels, it is very difficult to explore his subconscious.

In individual coaching or therapy, dissociation can manifest as:

- rational analysis of a situation (usually of its external details) without emotional awareness and insight

- lack of useful answers to questions about emotions; the client often offers different rational theories, memories or ideas instead (or very often answers "I don't know")

- difficulties in verbalizing emotions or maintaining awareness of an emotion

- a person cannot distinguish mature from immature emotions, i.e., appropriate ones from those that are inappropriate for a specific situation

- a person cannot recognize or verbalize unconscious memories. Sometimes a client rejects the idea that the root of the problem might be in a situation or circumstances that she cannot consciously remember. For example, one client told me: "Why do you ask me about my childhood? My childhood has nothing to do with how I feel! I am under stress because of how other people around me behave". This seems obvious to people who are not aware of their unconscious processes. When we learn to explore beneath the surface of our experience, we can find the reasons why people react so differently to similar circumstances.

- unawareness, or active rejection, of responsibility for one's own emotions, as a result of lack of consciousness of their underlying causes

- such people usually expect quick solutions, often hoping that others and/or external circumstances would change.

Sometimes it is easier to work with such clients through metaphors – symbolic images. However, this kind of work still requires them to, to some extent, give up conscious control and allow spontaneous associations, so difficulties can also occur.

If you recognize yourself in any of these descriptions, my primary recommendation is long-term work on building awareness of your body and emotions. Practice daily observation and detailed exploration of your emotions. You can find additional help in other approaches that intensify bodily consciousness, like meditation, dance, aromatherapy, massage, and bathing – activities that combine working on your physical body with a relaxed consciousness.

Layers of emotional experience

Our emotional states consist of several layers; just as our personalities consist of a number of "sub-personalities". Different parts of our consciousness will experience an intense situation differently. Often, one part of our personality will try to hide, suppress or protect another part: anger, for example, can cover fear, shame or guilt. Sadness can be expressed instead of anger by people who learned that they would be punished if they expressed anger. Blaming others is usually an automatic defense from guilt.

If we dissociate from our emotions, we can recognize only the most intense and most obvious ones, while staying unaware of all the emotional layers beneath. Thus, we see a given situation only from a limited point of view, which can motivate immature behavior and trigger more conflict. This is easier to notice in others, and most of us will do so with relish, but it can be difficult when it comes to ourselves.

Many of us have learned to suppress some emotions even before they become conscious. Thus, even when we want to explore them, due to this automatic suppression, we might feel like we are trying to grab a piece of soap in water. We might be momentarily aware of the emotion, but unable to stay focused, because in the next moment our defense mechanisms step in. The earlier the age of fragmentation, the more intense our defenses, the more difficult it is to recognize the patterns on which our personalities were built. We are immersed in them like fish in water. It is often easier to identify temporary emotional states, than those that prevail in our everyday experience.

Before the age of three, a child is not familiar with the spoken language well enough to think in the verbally-logical way of adults. Impressions and conclusions are made on emotional, not on intellectual level. Thus, those emotional impressions cannot be resolved and healed

36

by the rational mind. That is why simply reading a good book, or a rational insight into a problem is rarely enough to find solutions. Only approaches that include working with emotional experiences can provide long-term change. Since most crucial patterns and basic emotional impressions are created before the age of three, it is a big handicap to be unable to work on them due to a lack of emotional awareness.

Sometimes, change can be easier for people who, at first glance, appear overly sensitive and socially awkward, because they are usually more aware of their problems – meaning that they are not afraid to admit them to themselves. People who experience their fear, shame, insecurity – can be a big step closer to happiness than people who mask their feelings with rationality or artificial self-confidence.

Practice:

Choose something about yourself that is difficult for you to accept, something that you dislike about yourself and you would like to get rid of. Invest some time and effort to fully accept and acknowledge the emotions of that *part* of you (perhaps malice, envy, shame...). You might notice other arising emotions that conflict with the first one and seem to be trying to deny and suppress it. If you notice the emotion withdrawing or diminishing when you focus on it, "refresh" it from time to time by remembering the situation that triggered that emotion.

Ask that part of yourself what does it really want, what is its true motivation (perhaps feeling worthy, strength, approval...), and what stops it from fulfilling this motivation in a healthy way. Try to feel the age of that part of you; that is, at what age would such an emotion make sense: childhood, adolescence, or maybe young adulthood? Give as much love as you can to that part of yourself, then also spread love to other parts of you that dislike and oppose the part you started with.

In the beginning, facing such emotions can be unpleasant. However, you will notice the discomfort, and afterwards the emotions themselves, weaken as soon as you fully accept them. When that happens, you will be able to feel much more love and compassion for yourself and for others.

To resolve these emotions permanently, you will need to dissolve the original trauma, which is a much more difficult and complicated process. In the appendix of this book, you can find some basic instructions on how to work with your emotions. Although this is possible to do alone, it requires continual switching between rational thinking, (while you are guiding yourself through the process) and deep awareness of subtle feelings. As a participant of Soulwork training said: "trying to do it by yourself is like trying to repair your own tooth by yourself!". However, acceptance and love for your emotions is an important step that can bring a lot of relief.

Observing Our Feelings

At the root of much immature behavior is an urge to avoid unpleasant feelings. Practicing observing our feelings is the foundation of self-improvement - as well as being one of the most natural, simple and actually pleasant exercises of self-awareness. I cannot emphasize enough how important it is. You can practice this at any time, in most circumstances and situations. Not only you will not lose awareness of the world around you; it will probably improve.

Remember moments when you felt in great danger: probably you felt like time was running much slower, your focus sharpened and your actions became better coordinated. This is a spontaneous increase of awareness. We cannot stay in such a state for long, it is too tiring - but we can practice it consciously.

Just sit for 20 minutes a day and observe everything you feel, without analyzing, without focusing on isolated emotions. This is like standing in a river and feeling the flow, but not allowing the river to carry you away or trying to stop it. Try to go back to this awareness whenever you can during your daily tasks. With time, you will notice an increasing ability to recognize subtle emotional signals.

Such a simple exercise can have profound benefits:

- intimacy with your own feelings and increased self-acceptance. Accepting your feelings results in less fear of unpleasant ones (since you can experience that you can cope with them better than you thought), and in integrating many sub-personalities into a balanced whole;

- developing inner strength and trust in yourself; a feeling of peace and worthiness that can assist when facing unpleasant social situations and makes it easier to surmount the most difficult emotional crises of your life;

- functioning in the world with integrity, authenticity and centeredness, without pretense or exaggeration. Less need for masks and robotic conditioned reactions. This is the foundation of quality relationships and earning appreciation of emotionally mature people;

- quickly recognizing and clearly expressing subtle feelings and needs in communication with other people, even in situations in which most people lose their centeredness and allow outer influences to govern their behavior;

- recognizing subtle signals of other people through increased awareness of the details of mutual communication;

- deeper presence and awareness of the *now* and greater ability to learn from each situation, thus using every moment in life to its fullest;

- strengthening of intuition due to noticing and verbalizing subtle emotional signals;

- increased creativity for the same reason as above;

- increased ability to recognize and follow your physical needs (e.g. food, movement, rest, etc.), as well as to recognize the urge for specific activities, which can help you achieve a harmonious and fluid existence and an increase in productivity. When you listen to healthy messages of your body and feelings, it is hardly possible to be lazy! When I truly follow this principle, I often complete the greatest amount of work in the minimum amount of time, and even enjoy it. In contrast, rational self-control makes many types of work feel imposed or burdensome;

- easier application of any method of self-improvement, through better introspection and increased consciousness. This is especially helpful with systems focused on exploring memories and subconscious mind;

- increased self-honesty and dramatically reduced self-deception and thus unwanted behaviors;

- ability to recognize and enjoy pleasant feelings. (The more we are aware of all our feelings, the more we are aware of the pleasant ones too. People who suppress their emotions and are hyper-rational, are rarely able to fully enjoy even their moments of happiness);

- feeling independent of other people and circumstances; feeling better able to fulfill your needs within, instead of depending on others and projecting your responsibilities onto them.

- The results are therefore worth the effort and time invested! You can start immediately without any foreknowledge or preparations. You do not need a specific space, equipment or setting - all you need is yourself and motivation for long-term daily practice.

Our True Self

Human beings are capable of wonderful, deep, sophisticated emotions, inspiring and passionate love and joy. However, it is often difficult to stay in touch with these emotions for extended periods.

Small children experience reflections of themselves and their behavior only through feedback from their families. Emotional feedback from other people enables them to get in touch with their own emotions. If people around a child cannot see, recognize and appreciate that child's true being, that child has no foundation to do it alone. Thus, little by little, she will lose contact with her true self, even if she experiences no obvious or serious trauma. Similarly, as muscles atrophy if not used, our sense of self can also "atrophy". This is not the best expression though – who we are cannot truly atrophy – but if we lose our ability to be aware of and express our honest emotions, the consequences can seem this way.

When working with clients, we often explore which parts of themselves they have lost contact with. Usually, those are the gentlest, warmest aspects of the self, those parts that are most trusting to the world and to ourselves.

If you examine what hurts most when you feel belittled and criticized, you will probably feel that your true being is ignored and not taken into account, while some unimportant parts of your behavior are interpreted in all sorts of arbitrary ways.

Each of us seems to have infantile personality parts, which, based on prior experiences, might make us feel rejected and unappreciated even in situations when this is not realistic: for example when somebody else is praised; or when we are asked to do something that we do not feel comfortable about; or when we hear an opinion which is different from our own. Even such benign situations can trigger infantile emotions. It feels worse when somebody acts with direct arrogance and disrespect. In such moments, it can be very difficult to stay adult and not to respond in a similar manner – that is, to lose sight of the other's true being.

A specific trigger is not always needed to stimulate feelings of rejection. An environment lacking emotional awareness can be enough. Just being in contact with people who cannot truly see and appreciate themselves and others can weaken self-awareness in a small child and encourage him to grow up into a similar kind of person.

When you walk through a city, you can repeatedly revive that unpleasant experience and atmosphere. You meet people, even children, whose empty, cold or even scornful faces can motivate you to close up. In subtle ways, each of those encounters, even if you do not notice them individually, is a confirmation of your early experiences. If unexpressed, our true nature and deepest feelings can be forgotten.

We all have our life battles and sometimes we can feel that nobody sees or appreciates them. Sometimes it will be true. On the other hand, how often do we notice and appreciate the efforts of others? Very rarely. To expect that from ourselves and others is not realistic in this society, since few people learn how to do it.

Imagine living among people who truly see and accept you even if you are not perfect. How would you feel if you were able to accept other people in the same way?

It is unrealistic to expect that we or others could do so based on our rational minds only. We may like to think that others should take many things into consideration, but this is not so easy. It takes time for us and others to heal.

We cannot see and appreciate others if we reject parts of ourselves. I notice that sometimes when I strive to understand others, parts of me ask: "And what about you?" Sometimes I feel an irrational fear that if I truly respect others, I have to reject myself or accept inappropriate behavior. Such infantile fears are not in line with reality – but we should not ignore them either.

Sometimes you might want to act more mature than other people, so that you can feel superior. This does not resolve problems, it only covers them up.

Even when we feel that somebody really sees or accepts our deepest feelings, we can doubt their sincerity, or whether we deserve such acceptance. We might even suspect manipulation, if we have often experienced being emotionally manipulated or exploited.

A common obstacle in personal development is that this kind of dissociation is so normal that we hardly notice it. Sometimes, for a moment, we may become aware of this problem, yet when the crisis is over we easily fall back to an "it-could-be-worse" attitude. Why not "it could be better"?

No matter how much I would like that, I do not believe that it is possible to change your personality working on the rational level only. We need to focus within and heal through deep emotional experience. After that, we can practice awareness and action from the center of our being. It takes time to learn to act like this in everyday life – if for decades our true being had no contact with outer reality. Still, it is possible. Maybe you cannot even imagine how much beauty you can find in yourself once you start to search.

Achieving Permanent Change

Some people just lack confidence that they can change. They feel that their problems are either too difficult or too deep, or they are disappointed with the approaches they already tried. Even more often, they are inclined to lose motivation if a dramatic change does not occur in a month or two; sometimes they are even aware that they did not actually invest much effort into self-improvement, or that they did not practice the things they learned.

Very often, people practice exercises and techniques irregularly, e.g., just a few times in a week. After a few months, they usually decide that they are not satisfied with the results, as if the results can come just from knowing the method rationally. On the other hand, people who really invest effort into using newly learned skills, sometimes expect too large a change in a short period, and if this does not happen, their motivation quickly diminishes.

One of the most important things that I can say about personal development is: give yourself time! Emotional problems are often created at the very beginning of our lives, when the personality is still developing, and after that are usually reinforced for decades. From a neurological point of view, repeated behaviors – including repetitive thinking patterns - create neurological connections, which consequently make it easier to repeat the same thinking habits. It takes time and perseverance for new neurological links to be shaped and new ways of thinking adopted.

As when losing weight or learning new skills – playing a musical instrument, combat skills, creative writing or anything else, if you set a target date just few weeks or months ahead, not only will you be dissatisfied with the results but also with the process itself. Premature deadlines create pressure and feelings of failure and insufficiency, and - as with rapid diets – you soon return to old habits and old problems. It is much wiser to give yourself six months, a year or two, or more, depending on the problem, and to establish a regular routine. Create habits that are easier to maintain, perhaps even enjoy – for extended periods, even for a lifetime.

While working with clients, I noticed that change is especially difficult for people whose parents did not want them. They did not experience basic acceptance or welcome into this world, thus the very foundations of their self-image can be negative.

Similarly, some parents are disappointed with the sex of their child. These are mostly daughters, especially in older generations. Such children often carry feelings of rejection and guilt, not because of their behavior, which could be changed, but because of their bodies. Such people need to practice extended and intense support and love for themselves, to change these deeply imprinted images.

My experience in working individually with these people is that they usually notice big changes in toxic beliefs, or to emotions like guilt, anger or fear in specific contexts. However, for existential goals, like significant changes in personality, work or partnership, they need to change many deep convictions and emotional reactions - not just a few, as people usually hope. People with difficult pasts built such complexes during repeated trauma and unhealthy relationships. Healing requires more intense work.

A woman I will call Laura worked with me on her partnership issues, like feeling hurt by some details of her partner's behavior, occasional jealousy, suffering in times of separation etc. At first, we met twice a month, and later once a month. In the meantime, she worked alone with guided exercises.

Very soon, she started to notice increased self-confidence and no longer felt dependent on her partner's behavior. After a while, she started feeling less interested to continue her relationship, as she felt that her important wishes and needs were not fulfilled. Still, she decided not to force a break up, but to stay in the relationship as long as she felt a need for it, using that time to work on every emotional problem that would come out.

As time passed, she would often tell me that attraction was diminishing and that she was no longer sure how long her relationship might last. Soon after, she met another man with whom she was able to create a relationship that she describes as true intimacy and partnership, everyday magic, an experience that is almost hard to believe.

This is a beautiful – and realistic! – example of what can be achieved through long-term continuous work and sincerity to yourself. This approach requires more time and effort than some "magic pill" techniques, but in this way problems can be resolved at their roots, on the level of causes and not effects - just like being overweight cannot be resolved with lotions and pills, but by changing unhealthy habits.

Working on many levels

Permanent and significant results come through a combination of working with causes of issues, developing new levels of consciousness and perception, creating new emotional experiences and practicing different behaviors in everyday situations.

Some people tell me that their starting positions are far more difficult and complicated than most. They expect that I might have trouble understanding them, since I do not know exactly how they feel. If I talk about my current self, it is true that I have a positive attitude about myself. However, when I started working on my personal development, this was not true. When I look back at my past, I would say that my history was rather average, if I compare myself to other people. (Some people hardly believe me when I tell them how I perceived myself when I was a teenager.) However, my challenges motivated me to grow and learn. Considering that you are reading this book right now, it is probably true for you, too.

Psychological structures change slowly; most people need a sense of continuity, gradual transition from the known to the unknown, instead of dramatic changes. Some people consciously fear change, although many more people carry this fear on an unconscious level.

Our personalities consist of many parts, often called sub-personalities. Some of them are more and some less active, and some are hidden most of the time. Those parts of us also need time to reorganize and adjust to change. Some of them might resist change due to a fear of "ego-death", a fear that the current personality might be damaged or destroyed. For a similar reason – fear of losing the sense of identity we are used to – we might be afraid to reach spiritual experiences and intense intimacy with others.

I have tried and tested many personal development techniques and met quite a few people doing the same. In spite of all promises and glorious marketing, I do not know anyone who achieved a dramatic

46

change in a short time. Sometimes external circumstances change or temporary ecstatic states are achieved, but our basic sense of who we are in this world changes at a much slower pace.

People I worked with often tell me that their lives have fundamentally changed, but never after a few days or even weeks. Yet when they look back and remember the way they felt months before, they see significant changes. This goal is achievable, very inspiring and motivating, if we were not so used to our consumer society, with everything in instant packages, and if we were willing to invest our time and effort into personal change. Instead, most people try to use external means to achieve inner changes. Character development can only be achieved through effort and experience.

From time to time, "leaps" in improvement are possible, including important positive changes within short periods of time, but those are, in my opinion, the results of previous efforts which created the conditions for subsequent changes.

Sometimes, true and full confrontation with an external situation can bring many liberating insights and changes in perspective, so that some emotional problems may spontaneously heal and with them any need to create similar situations. For example, I have experienced that if I said aloud my opinion to people whose reactions I feared, I felt enormous relief and freedom to speak up. However, to do that, I needed to be aware of my emotions, true to myself and I needed to learn how to better react to external challenges. Thus, this kind of healing is also a result of long-term effort.

Results come easier and faster when we work with our unpleasant emotions before confronting real-life situations, but one without the other is not enough. Healing emotional patterns without checking the results in real life, or trying to change external circumstances without changing the deep beliefs that originally helped creating them, will rarely provide lasting results.

As with losing weight, accepting the fact that we cannot be liberated of our imperfections overnight is a key to true freedom. Just like in choosing a profession or a hobby, it is important to find satisfaction in the chosen method of personal development itself, not only in the result. It is an opportunity to practice enjoying the present moment and to love ourselves the way we are.

Allow changes to happen gradually, step by step, layer by layer, yet persistently for permanent results. A year of patience and discipline can often save a decade of useless effort. As some of my clients said: "I can hardly recognize the person I used to be!"

How to Stay Motivated?

Insufficient intensity and continuity of personal development are common reasons why many people feel that their efforts do not produce results. At first glance, this might look like a simple problem and that the solution is just some more will power (or the latest fad).

The underlying issues, however, might be one or more of the following:

- fear of confronting unpleasant or unknown beliefs or emotions;

- fear of endangering important relationships (many of our toxic beliefs were created so that we could maintain important relationships in toxic circumstances)

- fear of change and of the unknown;

- rebellious feelings that might make any attempt at discipline feel hostile and imposed. This is usually connected to previous experiences of being disciplined;

- following rigid schedules increases suppression and resistance (as opposed to feeling our natural rhythms);

- unconscious bonding to suffering.

Bonding to suffering is a complex and interesting idea, described by Eva Pierrakos in her book "Creating Union". The author wrote that, as children, to defend ourselves from pain, we can learn to take subtle pleasure in suffering. In extreme cases, the result can be masochism (or sadism, when pleasure is projected onto the suffering of others).

To some extent, this pattern is present in everyone and is manifested through finding pleasure in complaining, retelling unpleasant events, playing victim roles, etc. Note that much humor is about other people's pain. We may unconsciously fear that if we give up suffering, we will also lose whatever pleasure we gain from it (e.g. the pleasure many people gain from complaining).

You might want to resolve some of these issues by searching for their causes - possible unpleasant experiences that triggered those patterns. However, some of them are so normal (e.g. resisting pressure and discipline) that it might make little sense to search for specific situations in which those patterns originated.

Apart from those emotional obstacles, there are simpler ones, e.g. forgetting, lack of time or focus due to the external circumstances. These, however, can also be ways to rationalize your unconscious self-sabotage. You might feel guilty or ashamed if you take time for yourself by saying, "No" to others (who afterwards can *comment* about your personal development). If you would not feel guilty or shameful, you could schedule some time for yourself, and explain to your family why this is important to you. Mention some benefits for them, too. People will be most tolerant to changes in your behavior, if they perceive how they can benefit from them. Strange, isn't it?

We can gradually lose motivation to improve ourselves if we do not know what the reward is – we may not be familiar enough with feelings of freedom, ease, love and other life changes that we could achieve. If you do not have a good idea of your reward, your motivation can suffer.

Some ways you can motivate yourself are:

- basic and most important: remind yourself over and over again, and try to imagine yourself with all the beautiful results and feelings you could achieve with persistent practice;

- use "negative motivation": imagine how your life and health would look like in five or ten years if nothing changes;

- choose the approach and exercises that you enjoy most, which will motivate you because of the process itself, not only because of results;

- if you feel resistance, admit it and take time to explore it;

- practice daily. Some people prefer schedules, others are more motivated by flexibility (although this won't be practical for very busy people);

- list the ideas you find most important and the exercises you like. Remind yourself by regularly rereading the list;

- reward yourself after specific periods of committed practice, perhaps two weeks or a month (avoid rewards like junk food or things that you know are not good for you);

– remind yourself that the more you learn from any situation and the more effort you invest every day, there is less chance of a serious crisis or disease.

Setting Boundaries

Many writers suggest ideal behaviors which people should strive to develop. Many people want to live up to spiritual ideals such as helping others, kindness, generosity and sharing.

They often forget, however, that most people they meet will be at a rather low level of emotional maturity and relationship awareness. People who live in fear, or with low awareness of the feelings and needs of others, cannot fully respect other people's boundaries. Some people will consciously take advantage of perceived weaknesses or compliance of others. Some will not do this on purpose, but will find numerous justifications. Thus, if you try to be nice and help others, you may find that other people will soon start expecting it and asking for it, and in this way drain your time and energy. Such parasitic relationships lack balance and true pleasure.

You do not owe your time, love, or even friendship to anybody. Those are rather abstract terms, so we might be confused about setting boundaries and remembering what we want. You might feel more guilt refusing requests for your time than for your money. Our parents probably did not give money to anyone - but perhaps they wasted their time and energy on people they disliked, to avoid offending them. We may have learned indirectly, or even after direct instructions, to waste time in the same way.

I am not suggesting isolating yourself and only doing what is profitable for you. Being a part of a friendly community, spending time together and helping each other can be a beautiful, rewarding experience. Many communities, however, have rather rigid rules, unhealthy expectations and pushy communication habits. It is up to you to create a balance between being friendly and compassionate, and taking care of yourself.

Sometimes the best way to help people can be to push them away, not to allow them to cling to us and waste our time and energy. In this way, we help people face themselves and their needs, find their own strength and develop independence. In contrast, serving their needs might only make them feel that it pays to be dependent. When we set boundaries, we express respect for and confidence in other people's strength and responsibility.

Even if you do not see anything unpleasant in some people, maybe you will not be attracted to them as potential friends. There is nothing wrong with this and you need not feel guilty by refusing to spend your time with them. It is important to understand that love and respect for others does not necessarily mean being at their disposal.

According to Deborah Tannen (author of "*You Just Don't Understand*"), women are more in danger of neglecting their boundaries. This is partly because of a feminine tendency to maintain harmony and avoid conflict, and partly because our society expects women to give more and values their time less than that of men. Many people will find it easier to ask women for their time or services for free, than to ask the same of men.

Many people, especially helping professionals, have problems with asking to be paid for their work. They may prefer not to have to ask, or to try requesting donations. This might be a solution in a community of emotionally mature people. Yet most people in our society have not developed a sense of balance in giving and receiving, or they are too afraid of losing money to pay as much as you think your work deserves.

If you depend on donations, you can feel exhausted, depreciated and exploited, not to mention problems paying your bills. Money is a practical way to exchange goods and services with clarity and balance. People with limiting beliefs about money might criticize you for this attitude or try to induce guilt in you. They may call you a fraud if you do not provide free services. An interesting question is, would they give their own work away for free?

Adult boundaries

Mature, responsible communication does not necessarily mean making other people feel good and avoiding hurt. Often, avoiding honesty about our thoughts and feelings only postpones conflict and makes it worse.

For example, if we use lies or excuses trying to avoid unwanted requests, instead of saying "No" directly, those requests may well continue. Other people will not become aware of our true feelings and if

54

we hope they would somehow intuit how we feel, we fool ourselves. People can distort reality in many ways, and are usually much more focused on their desires than yours. They may repeat their requests more frequently, until the situation escalates to either open conflict or avoidance and leaves a "sour taste in the mouth".

Here is a basic rule: you are responsible for your own behavior, not for the feelings of others. That means: if you do your best to communicate with respect and integrity, there is no reason to feel guilt even if the other person feels hurt and perhaps blames you.

Setting boundaries is equally important in an intimate partnership as in other relationships. Many people burden their partners with high expectations and needs, and therefore do not respect their boundaries. On the other hand, some people may give their partners too much space and avoid expressing their requirements. They may call this love, while acting out of fear and neediness. Then suppressed frustration builds up until it either explodes or slowly erodes trust and intimacy. So why not to stop this process at the beginning?

Such lack of honesty is often due to a fear of abandonment. Many people learned early in their lives that, if they want to be loved, they cannot be who they are, or that love means that the needs of others are more important than their own.

How can we recognize healthy boundaries and when do we disregard them? Pay attention to your subtle emotions and translate them into words as best you can. If you do not listen to your emotions, sooner or later you might get psychosomatic warning signals.

Be aware that your boundaries might not be compatible with other people's. This is normal and there is no need to blame anyone. Through honest negotiations, you can explore what sort of relationship you want in such a case. If some people avoid honest negotiations by criticizing, blaming or giving you silent treatment, reconsider how much time you want to spend with them.

Anger and aggression

If someone threatens our personal boundaries, it is not a good enough reason to react angrily, with either active or passive aggression. Anger and blame often signal suppressed fear and unresolved guilt, which we must accept and understand in order to deal with them efficiently.

It is important to differentiate between decisiveness and aggression, as well as between permissiveness and compassion. This may be difficult for people who were taught to suppress their needs and feelings. They may react out of guilt mixed with fear and anger, if forced to set boundaries. This often occurs after a period of hiding emotions, repressing anger and accumulating resentment.

Some people defend their personal boundaries decisively, yet also aggressively through blaming or criticizing others, even for the smallest of problems. The more aggression, the more suppressed fear and guilt you can expect. Such people are likely to have been badly insulted or hurt in childhood and decided to fight for themselves, but from a stance of "Do unto others before they do unto you".

This attitude often comes from fear that they could not protect themselves without attacking or degrading others. Often they had strong role models for such behavior. This is neither self-love nor self-esteem, rather a different way of expressing the same problem.

Assume that people do not act with a conscious intention to insult or hurt you, except when openly aggressive or manipulative. If you understand that most people have not developed their consciousness of values and feelings of others, you need not react with anger (only irritation).

It is usually inappropriate to express desires or requests with anger and accusations. Otherwise, we risk pushing people into defensiveness, damaging potential quality relationships.

It is crucial to recognize, define and explain your boundaries, needs and desires to others early in relationships. If you avoid this, you may end up accumulating resentment. Most people did not learn to be sufficiently aware of others' nonverbal signals and cannot recognize indirect warnings. In such a case, you might delay expressing your needs until an emotional or even physical crisis occurs.

Notice what stops you from calmly explaining to other people what you want and what is not acceptable to you, without fear, blame and anger. If you avoid making your boundaries clear, you will probably feel uncomfortable and limited in your communications. This may even lead you to push people away - blaming them for your discomfort rather than acknowledging your own emotions.

The more you disrespect yourself and your needs, the more you are likely to disrespect other people and their needs, even if only inside your mind.

It is good to remember this when questioning your own behavior and demands. It is easier to sense when our own boundaries are threatened; it might be challenging to recognize when we intrude on other people's boundaries. If we do not love ourselves, we may feel inferior when we recognize our faults and inappropriate behavior. Thus, we can be motivated to avoid questioning our motives. The more we accept ourselves, the more we can accept -and correct- our mistakes.

We no longer live in medieval conditions in terms of physical security, but our society is still both verbally and emotionally violent. Even if we do not express hostility, we may desire to. Fear keeps (some) people from being openly rude, rather than appreciating or understanding others. Violence may remain in our thoughts or we may express it behind people's backs. We may accept this as normal, or justify it in similar ways like people in the Middle Ages accepted and justified physical violence. To some extent, we are still in the Middle Ages, even if only mentally. To change something outside of ourselves, we must first recognize it within.

Self-criticism will not help us change how we relate to others. It can worsen the problem, causing inner conflict and suppression. Suppressed parts of ourselves then become stronger and more violent, seeking attention and recognition.

To recognize other people's pain, we must first recognize our own. To understand how we hurt others, we must first become aware of how we hurt ourselves. We hurt ourselves every day, living lives we do not enjoy, remaining in surroundings we do not like, poisoning and neglecting our bodies, searching for something or somebody to save us from ourselves. This cannot change until we stop believing that people or circumstances dictate the choices we make and are hence responsible for us.

Points to ponder:

Do you agree to do things for others without checking if you truly want to?

Do you spend time with people because you feel good with them, because of routine, or because you cannot say "No"?

Do you ignore and avoid expressing uncomfortable feelings until they become unbearable? How do you act then?

What stops you from expressing discontent the moment you feel it? Do you think something like "this is not so important", or "I love this person too much to be bothered with such little things", "it is stupid to complain about something so insignificant", or are you simply afraid of other people's anger, criticism or ridicule?

How do you feel when someone says "No" to something you desire or request? Do you feel that either you or other people should not express different opinions or choices?

How do you feel when you ask for, receive or give money? Do you feel guilt or try to induce it?

Do you feel responsible for other people's emotional reactions if they do not agree with your boundaries?

Do you expect your partner to always fulfill your needs in the way you wish?

Practice:

Pay attention to situations when you may ignore your discomfort. Observe your emotions when you feel discontent, or when you are scared to express your boundaries. To work with difficult emotions, you can use the "Exploring Emotions" process in the appendix of this book.

Examine your expectations of other people, especially of your family, partner and friends. How do you feel when they do not do what you want? Do you resent and blame them, or can you negotiate in friendly ways?

If you have just started a relationship, or if you want to improve an existing relationship, list what you want or what bothers you, things that you would like the other person to pay attention to. Discuss this with the other person. Inspire him or her to do the same. (Good luck!) Pay attention to how this person reacts. If good communication is not possible, check why you stay in that relationship.

Healthy Family Relationships

Children need to trust important adults. This need is so strong that it is at the root of many traumas and limiting beliefs: they are created as a way for children to continue trusting their parents. Besides the need to trust, there is also a need to love and to be loved, so small children create many defense mechanisms to continue loving difficult yet important people.

Children under three years of age are extremely dependent of their parents. Any awareness that they cannot rely on the parents is too frightening to accept. Therefore, they spontaneously and unconsciously find justifications for their parents. If parents act immaturely, children can take responsibility by creating toxic beliefs about themselves. Beliefs like: "I am not good enough", "Something is wrong with me", "My feelings are not important" can become rooted in the foundations of personality and affect adult lives. As adults, we can feel them acutely, especially in situations that remind us of the original disappointments in which those beliefs were created (e.g., criticism, violence, ridicule, etc.).

For example, a parent may shout at, insult or ignore a child because of small mistakes, especially if the parent is already frustrated by other life circumstances. The child can either recognize that the parent is acting in an immature, unjustified and unreasonable manner, or trust the parent and conclude that the mistake justifies such a strong reaction.

Older children could feel safer recognizing their parents' imperfections, but children who are under three years old cannot. Small children lack experience and perspective to recognize immaturity, so they will blame themselves, thus creating a belief that even small mistakes are unacceptable. It is very difficult, if not impossible, to be perfect, especially if you are a young child and the rules keep changing. The next step for children is to convince themselves that they are not good enough and that something is wrong with them. Older children may try to defend themselves from such feelings with rage and spite, but these are just defense mechanisms, not solutions.

Age regression

Once deep beliefs are created, infantile emotions can be awakened by similar situations, for example, when somebody criticizes us, ignores us or puts us down. This happens because, unconsciously, our brain compares new situations to similar past experiences and their outcomes.

Sometimes, little details are sufficient – the tone of the voice, facial expression, a specific word or gesture – to remind us of early situations. Then buried feelings related to those situations arise from the unconscious. This is called "age regression" – emotionally returning to a younger age. Sometimes fear, shame or sorrow might come out, and sometimes they are instantly hidden by defensive anger or spite. When such strong feelings arise, it is very difficult to distance oneself from them and assess a situation from a realistic, objective perspective. This is how adult, healthy people can get sucked into foolish, irrational conflicts.

This is why some people feel that violence and disrespect are normal or not worth reacting to. Some people might admit that they feel bad, but are afraid to react, or will blame themselves and their behavior, as they did when they were children. Others may react with childish rage and desire to punish someone. Few people can stay calm, feeling good about themselves, trying to understand aggressive people while calmly stating their points of view.

Over and over again, when I work with people, together we discover the deep beliefs that they created during childhood events, for example, reckless statements of parents: "You were a mistake", or "I don't love you. Do you love me?". Parents may have told their children that they stayed married only because of them. Some parents were absent because of work or emotional unavailability, some were extremely strict ... children under such stress can create deep toxic beliefs about their personality and worth.

We can deal with most adults who "push our buttons" by avoiding them or letting them know that their behavior is unacceptable, but with children, this is harder and takes time. Children can trigger our suppressed feelings through their uninhibited and demanding behavior, through their needs and persistence, through their experimenting with behaviors that are not all mature and pleasant.

When we are confronted with feelings that we do not know how to deal with, with demands and situations to which we never learned to respond appropriately, we will try to find the fastest solution to get rid of unpleasant tension. We automatically use the most familiar solutions – ones our parents used to make us easier to control. In this way, we can teach our own children to feel disproportionate fear and guilt. This is how unhealthy patterns are carried over from generation to generation.

Respectful discipline

Discipline is important and justified as a tool to teach children about the needs and boundaries of other people, instead of allowing them to grow up with the expectation that everyone should comply with their demands. Some parents fear that limitations or rejections might hurt their children – but a true mistake would be to discipline in insensitive or humiliating ways.

Discipline can and should include love and respect. There are better ways to influence children instead of shouting, threatening and beating, and many books give advice about how to do this. It is important to treat children in similar ways that we treat adults: set similar boundaries, and with similar respect; however, not with similar expectations. Children easily forget requests, they may not understand or reason like adults and they may have less control of their impulses. This does not mean that they are disobedient or that they do not respect you.

Family as a system

Most people seem to sense what is healthy and what is unhealthy in family relationships. Yet most families have traditions of unhealthy patterns and imposed guilt, which hinder family members from acting in ways they feel are right. Guilt can prevent us from objectively evaluating our behavior, as well as the actions of other family members.

Martyn Carruthers (founder of Soulwork Systemic Coaching) says that families are *emotional systems*. Like all living systems, families try to maintain a stable balance (homeostasis), and if a part of a system becomes dysfunctional, other parts will try to compensate.

Children are the most sensitive and receptive parts of family systems, and will attempt to compensate for threats to family stability. They might do this by accepting responsibilities that they are not ready for. Some children redirect family activity and attention by exhibiting problematic behavior, including expressing taboo emotions or forbidden urges.

Children often express feelings and impulses that one or both parents deny or avoid expressing (e.g. sexuality or anger). This can continue into adulthood. For both children and their families, such compulsions can be unpleasant and incomprehensible; children often learn to feel shameful and guilty because of such *systemic* behavior.

People have often told me that if they tried to hide unpleasant emotions in the presence of a small child, the child would start to cry or become restless and irritable.

From time to time, parents who are confused by their children's depression, fear or aggression, claim that there is no reason for this. In many such cases, the parents suppress emotions. Children are much more observant and sensitive than parents imagine. They notice non-verbal behavior and might pick up even the emotions that you successfully hide from yourself.

When parents complain about their difficult children, I prefer to work with the parents. As parents change their self-images, their views of past experiences and finally feel relief, they often tell me that the children, without any apparent reason, changed their behavior. Some feedback from parents I worked with is that their children now communicate more calmly or study without stress.

Many parents have irrational, compulsive urges, yet expect their children to control their own urges without having received any guidance. Some parents do not recognize unhealthy behaviors until they become intolerable, and many more do not know how to respond to them. They may ignore or justify even obvious problematic behaviors until it becomes a crisis or is made obvious by an outside stimulus (e.g. a complaint from a social worker). Then they often blame their children for causing such problems.

Another common reason for not resolving problems is shame of being labeled as sick or dysfunctional. It is important to understand that it is not shameful to have emotional problems. They are quite common and normal, as opposed to a perfect outside appearance that most people try to project.

Principles of a healthy family

Here are some basic principles of healthy family behavior the way I see it:

• Healthy and mature adults take responsibility for their own feelings, actions and life circumstances. They do not expect their children to defend them and to support them emotionally.

• Healthy and mature parents encourage their children to develop their own identities, and to separate from their parents to create independent lives. Eventually, both parents and children can relate to each other as mature and responsible people.

• Healthy children respect their parents, their parents' history and decisions, but focus on their own lives and their own children. They are aware that their parents are adults who can choose to live their lives responsibly.

Some parents expect their children's gratitude, "paying off a debt". Sometimes this means that, in return, children should sacrifice their own needs, even their own personalities. Mature, responsible parents understand that children are not in debt to them and especially that children are not obliged to sacrifice their happiness for their parents' benefit.

Giving birth to a child, as well as investing time, energy and money in a child are priceless gifts. A healthy adult person will feel gratitude and respect for the gift of life. However, as soon as parents start to demand specific expressions of gratitude, especially if they demand unnecessary sacrifices, life stops being a gift freely given, and becomes a trade and possibly blackmail. For children of such parents, this "gift" can become a heavy burden, having to live with the expectation that it has to be repaid someday. This can result in heavy guilt and low self-esteem.

In the past, when parents could not easily control the number and timing of pregnancies, it was rather understandable that some of them might resent their lives being burdened by unplanned parental responsibilities. With contraception now so easily available, better parent-child relationships became possible: based on appreciation rather than resentment. Perhaps we should thank the inventors of contraceptives for this huge change in society. Contraception did not only enable women to become more independent, it also assisted in changing how parents perceive their children. This had huge consequences for the emotional maturity in societies.

When children or adult people are under pressure to fulfill their parents' emotional needs, it causes suffering, emotional disorders and relationship problems. This burden may be carried over from generation to generation and can be difficult to change.

It is natural that young adults give priority to their own lives and families (their partners and children). Taking responsibility for their parents' needs, feelings and happiness, sacrificing themselves, trying to make parents happy ... this means perceiving parents as weak children instead of responsible adults. I do not claim that people should abandon sick and old parents – but some physically healthy parents expect their offspring to neglect their own families to take care of them. Healthy people will give necessary help to disabled parents and still see them as responsible adults.

Nicholas, a man in his fifties, suffered from severe depression. He had dedicated most of his life to the demands and needs of his mother, who also suffered from depression. Since he was a small child, she had persuaded him that his behavior was the main cause of her depression. Nicholas believed her to such an extent that, even as an adult, he was convinced of his guilt. He spoke of his mother with admiration and described her almost as a saint. Unfortunately, since he was strongly against exploring his relationship with his mother, there was no way for him to move forward. His descriptions of his relationship with his children were very one-sided, although I would expect that his children carried similar unhealthy responsibilities and guilt as he did.

Relationships with children

Blaming can become a habit. Adults who are irritated by a child's behavior, may automatically conclude that the child is at fault, instead of checking the background of their own feelings, or possible causes of the child's behavior. Many adults treat children with little respect, because children are less experienced and have less ability to express themselves verbally. Some adults communicate in cold or commanding ways, disregarding children's emotional needs, when they should be communicating and treating children as human beings who are valuable and sensitive, even if inexperienced about life.

More experience does not necessarily mean that adults are always right. This is more obvious when we look back at the not-so-distant past, when children's spontaneity was opposed by rigid and toxic beliefs of grown-ups – who, of course, assumed that they were right. Many girls were punished for wanting to run and climb trees, while many boys were humiliated for showing feelings. Even today, similar attitudes are common, perhaps on subtler levels and about smaller details (for example, forcing a child to eat more than his stomach can hold).

I like to differentiate between wisdom and rational knowledge. Wisdom is a form of intelligence deeply connected to and cooperating with feelings, while knowledge refers to collected data. From this point of view, children sometimes even have an advantage over adults, since they can be more aware and open to their honest feelings. Their handicap is the inability to consider a lot of information which can only be acquired through experience and learning. Children also lack the vocabulary to describe what is going on in their minds.

If we talk to someone in a foreign language, we might feel uncomfortable and insecure, not because our thoughts were inferior, but because we cannot find the best words to express them. Children can feel in a similar way when in front of self-assured and verbally skilled adults. Grown-ups often use this fact to their advantage, not considering consequences for children. Children whose opinions and reasoning were dismissed in patronizing ways, or who were laughed at, can later in life have problems trusting and expressing themselves.

Sometimes, healing includes not only resolving traumatic experiences, but also the consequences of subtler circumstances (even those that might appear positive). Parents may enjoy feeling powerful and important because they have more experience than their children. For some people this might be their only chance to feel powerful. Others, with best intentions, may have too high expectations from children at certain ages, or expect their children to be "special".

Children often idealize parents who present themselves as powerful and smart - they admire and wish to fulfill their parents' expectations. I have met people whose unhealthy patterns were caused by such circumstances. They felt unable to fulfill expectations, never good enough compared to their apparently perfect parents. Often they were attracted to potential partners who impressed them, but with whom they felt unworthy.

In those areas of life in which we spent most of our energy and time, it might be difficult for us to allow our children to be different, to live their own lives and beliefs. People who focus on material goods often put material demands on their children, while children's ideas and beliefs are less important. Intellectual parents might be less interested in formalities and material goods, but may not accept their children's different ideas and beliefs. If something is important to us, we are likely to want the important people in our life to agree with us, so we might attempt to rigidly control our children or give them conditional love. (E.g. "I will only love you if you do as I want").

Communication skills

Books about child psychology and upbringing are increasingly popular. As with other forms of personal development, however, techniques can be used superficially to achieve external results, without much understanding of the meaning and purpose of a particular approach. Some people, on the surface, may seem to apply appropriate communication skills, but without truly understanding children; they just hope for fast results. Their nonverbal communication – especially their tone of voice and facial expressions – will still show a lack of patience and respect (especially if the results are not as desired).

Children are generally more sensitive than adults and will be more influenced by nonverbal signals and emotional energy than by words alone. If non-verbal signals conflict with spoken words, it is natural that the child's motivation to cooperate will not increase. The parent often attributes this lack of success to the child's character.

For example, a commonly suggested communication method is called "*I-messages*". Instead of complaints starting with "You" (e.g. "Why don't you listen to me" or "You are so lazy!") parents are encouraged to talk about their feelings and wishes starting with "I". For example, "When you don't tidy your room, I feel I have to do all the work and I feel frustrated". This can work beautifully if parents speak to their children with appreciation and sensitivity. However, if parents use such sentences "mechanically" while their bodies radiate impatience or scorn, children will react to that impatience and scorn, not to the words.

Some parents might turn such an approach into manipulation and victim games, for example, "If you don't tidy your room, I will be so sad!" This appears to be a correct form of an *I-message*, but implies that the parents are unable to deal with their emotions, so the children should feel responsible. A huge amount of this message is communicated by body and tonality, not by words. This might motivate some children to cooperate out of guilt, but there will be long-term consequences such as loss of trust and mutual respect.

What is the root?

Most parents believe that they give the best they can to their children and to a certain extent, they are right. If children start to behave in an unwanted or unhealthy manner, this is usually attributed to either the influence of other children, or the media.

There is more and more awareness about the importance of the first three years of a child's life. The influence of peers and the media becomes important in subsequent years, after the most important years of character development are over. However, even when these external influences become stronger, they cannot shape a child's personality as quickly and powerfully as those early, unconscious inputs. Peers and media mostly encourage pre-existing elements in a child's experiences and feelings.

I want to emphasize that a child's personality is not only created by what is present and experienced in life, but also by what is missing. Parents may not understand this, if they perceive children as a kind of "tabula rasa" (blank page) who cannot miss things they never even knew.

Many people who start exploring their feelings and subconscious soon discover that when they were children, they needed higher quality love than they received. Parents might not be mature enough to love their children unconditionally, or might be limited by society (jobs and commuting time, urban environment with its dangers and not enough space for children to play etc.). Some unpleasant beliefs and poor character traits could be developed as a consequence of that lack of unconditional love. It is interesting to ponder where such need for love comes from, if we never experienced it? Perhaps we carry within us some sort of memory of what we truly are?

In all human relationships, regardless of age, most nonverbal communication is perceived and processed unconsciously. It influences relationships through subliminal impressions, rather than conscious evaluation. When children are very young, nonverbal impressions are much more significant than words, especially as children cannot yet understand words as well as adults. The influence of those non-verbal impressions underlies many later behavioral problems that parents do not understand and deny responsibility for. Some problems do not manifest until adolescence, when children find themselves unprepared for independence and mature partnership.

Points to ponder:

If you are a parent, do you feel that you truly know your child? Do you regularly "update" your perception of your child, and the way you behave towards her, as she grows older? Or did your perception "get stuck" in some early stage of her life? Does your child trust you enough to open up and talk about herself?

Do you respect your child and his emotional wisdom? Do you notice how your child reacts to your behavior? How do you account for unwanted elements of your child's behavior?

If your child keeps expressing "unreasonable" emotions, or behaviors that you cannot logically explain, check if you have any suppressed emotions that you might be avoiding to come to terms with. Is it possible to find the explanation for your child's behavior in those suppressed emotions?

Do you expect your children to be your "extensions" or that "you will live on through them"? Why is that so? Do you have any wishes or goals that you have not achieved and expect your child to do it for you?

Is it acceptable to you if your child lives an independent life? Is it acceptable if your child is happier than you are? Is it all right if you are happy and independent from your own parents?

Do you need your children to express and prove their gratitude? Do you feel that you have to "pay off" some debt to your own parents, for giving birth to and raising you?

Do you respect your needs and personal boundaries within your family? Do you respect the boundaries of other members of your family?

Do you blame your parents for not being perfect and not being able to give you what you needed? Or do you tend to defend and idealize them? Both are signs of unresolved emotions.

Practice:

Ask your partner and friends about their opinions of your relationship with your family.

Express your points of view and feelings to family members with whom you would like to improve your relationship. Check if you feel any obstacles to do so. If you feel fear or guilt, use the process "Exploring Emotions" in the appendix of this book.

Make an effort to improve the quality of your communication with your children. Read books, attend workshops (many organizations give free workshops for parents), and invest time and creativity in exploring better ways to communicate than those you learned as a child.

Little Prince and Daddy's Princess

If you talk to people who lack knowledge about psychology, about how to raise children or of love and respect children need, you might hear something like this: "I don't agree with pampering children. My father used to beat me up and that taught me right from wrong, while I know people whose parents gave them everything and were always there for them, and they became spoiled brats in adult bodies".

Although many people complain about a lack of parental love, some people received too much attention, although immature and needy attention, instead of responsible parenting. Soulwork Systemic Coaching recognizes patterns of emotional incest and their consequences. Soulwork practitioners call this syndrome "Little Prince" and "Daddy's Princess".

This pattern is not only about immature love and unhealthy permissiveness. A key issue is that a parent loves a child as if the child was a partner, expecting the child to fulfill the role and behavior of a partner. This usually happens if parents did not learn how to fulfill their needs for partnership and love through quality communication and respect – and this is common. This pattern is especially dangerous if a child lives with a separated or widowed parent of the opposite sex, but it is common enough in seemingly stable families, if there is no mature love between parents.

When parents fight through their children, trying to make them take sides, it can be very confusing and frightening. Children can start to see the world as an unsafe place and develop distrust in people – or stop trusting their own inner guidance. Some of those children develop chronic internal conflict.

Children over the age of seven can handle such circumstances better. If children are under seven and the most important people in their lives tell them contradictory things, or even talk badly about each other, they will create strong defense mechanisms – so-called masks, or false identities, each of which tries to please – and love – one of the conflicted adults.

A client that I will call Mark had a rude, verbally aggressive father and a passive mother who played a victim role. Both parents grew up in rough families focused on bare material survival, in which children were more numbers than individuals. To please his father, Mark developed a cold, insensitive and ironic side that would break through from time to time. At other times, he would act as the gentle, sensitive man that his mother wanted. To resolve this pattern, it was necessary for him to recognize the deep needs that motivated both of those behavior styles. He also needed to become aware of his true feelings and wishes, and to practice expressing them.

The key issue of emotional incest is that a parent turns to a child as a source of partner love, and unconsciously or even consciously expects the child to fulfill the parent's emotional needs, to replace an adult partner. Usually, although not always, immature parents bond to children of the opposite sex. At the same time, the other parent is often rejected and alienated, so he/she gives up communication and perhaps devotes time to another child. Sometimes the bonded parent and child start treating the other parent as their child (especially if the other parent is sick or addicted).

Emotional support on a partnership level – sharing feelings and responsibilities, mutual decision making, raising children together (if a parent and child together take care of other children and/or the other parent)... is suitable for a partnership between two adults, not for a relationship between a parent and a child. Children in such circumstances may feel that they cannot live up to expectations, and might become anxious, perfectionist, controlling or feel chronically inadequate. Some children, on the other hand, might enjoy this special position and power, and expect privileged treatment thereafter.

Consequences of emotional incest

Besides jealousy and competition between children of the same sex, this pattern leads to other predictable consequences. Children feel forced to hide their own identity to satisfy the parent's requirements. A boy can become very responsible, capable and intelligent, but emotionally immature, while a girl can develop either a similar pattern or that of a "helpless princess". If the father wanted her to stay childish, she might learn to hide her intelligence and manipulate her way to attention and adoration, since she does not dare to express herself openly.

A child might try to become "special" and perfect to satisfy the parent, or (usually in puberty) rebellious and spiteful, or develop a conflict between those two sides of personality.

Some common consequences for such children are (according to Martyn Carruthers):

- learning disabilities (attention deficit, caused by avoiding emotional awareness)

- withdrawal or exaggerated bonding to others

- lack of trust, sympathy or motivation for intimacy

- lack of self-esteem and self-control

Possible delayed consequences for adult offspring:

- expectation of adoration and parental behavior from a partner

- either overly responsible or avoids responsibility

- fear of being controlled

- avoiding committed partnership through solitude, intellectualism or promiscuity

- guilt prevents happiness

- lack of personal identity and integrity

A parent who bonds to a child in such a way, will usually try to preserve this bond even when the child grows up. Parents might use manipulation, guilt and buying love (through favors, expensive gifts, financial help and so on) to keep the offspring focused on them. Physical disease might motivate the offspring to stay close, so such parents might unconsciously sabotage their health out of fear of being abandoned. The parent might be especially jealous of the son or daughter's intimate partners and might try to turn the child against them.

The guilt of a child who was in such a way expected to "pay back" for being born and raised, in combination with the guilt of taking someone else's position in the family, is usually too deep and too strong to be consciously explored. People brought up in this way may consider manipulation, lack of boundaries or egotism to be normal and justified, and may rarely set boundaries or search for independent happiness.

We find this pattern to be more common between mothers and sons, than between fathers and daughters or other combinations. One reason might be that, in the past, men were usually more distant from families, looking for recognition and approval outside of them, while women were bonded and limited to their families, seeking emotional support within them, since it was rarely possible to get it from husbands. Lately, as men became more family-oriented, father-daughter bonding became more common.

Very often, women whom I have worked with, confirmed that they experienced their partner to be subordinated to his family, especially to his mother. Symptoms can include:

- spending too much time with his mother and expecting the wife or girlfriend to accompany him and approve of it

- allowing the mother to be overly and sometimes rudely involved in partnership decision making

- allowing the mother to criticize or humiliate her daughter-in-law, even to try to turn the grandchildren against her.

Partnership with a parent-bonded person

If you are in an intimate relationship with such a person, you already know the consequences to your family and partnership. Ask your partner to imagine how he would feel if he put his own life and family first. Ask your partner about her feelings of owing something to her parent and how she would feel if she stopped trying to make the parent happy and expressed her true feelings to him. Expect guilt, incredulity and justifications in favor of parents (e.g. "my mother/father did so much for me" ... "it's normal that people care for their families" and similar responses).

If your partner is parent-bonded, examine your own emotional patterns; that is, why were you romantically attracted to this kind of person in the first place. People with this kind of a syndrome are often strongly romantically attracted to potential partners with complementary patterns. In their partnership, they might switch between the roles of parent and child.

In time, they may become irritated by the partner's behavior ("You are just like my father!") or feel guilt or depression about leaving their parents. Then they may emotionally withdraw and sabotage partnership intimacy. This can lead to divorce, victim games, therapy ... or focusing on a child as a partner substitute, which carries the pattern to the next generation.

If you want to change such a situation, first take responsibility for yourself and your happiness. If your partner definitely does not want to change, (I suggest that, before you make this conclusion, you both seek counseling with an expert), ask yourself why you stay in such a situation. What are you afraid of, or what have you learned to accept as normal? Consider how will your life look like in five or ten years, if the situation is not remedied? How might you feel if you invested that time in working on your personal development instead?

These questions can open deep insights, not only about your relationships patterns and self-esteem, but also about your financial independence. Women especially might feel limited in this area as they may face realistic limitations, such as taking care of children, employers' reluctance to hire single mothers, or lack of education and work experience due to the time invested in motherhood.

Yet, we are even more limited by our habitual beliefs about ourselves and our abilities, or about money and life in general. Resolving financial issues may demand a deep change of your sense of identity, of how you perceive reality, and a consistent change in behavior. This cannot be done in a couple of weeks or months, so give yourself time and be patient with yourself.

Need for parental love

Another toxic pattern is expecting parental love from a child. Parents may unconsciously hope that in a relationship with a child they can experience the love that was lacking in their early family. Parents who grew up with little support sometimes feel that a baby might be the only person who accepts them and loves them the way they are, the only person who they can ever be truly close to.

Consequently, a parent might feel an urge to earn, or even buy, approval and love from a child. An expectation that the child will take care of the parent's feelings is even more present than in the previously discussed emotional incest. This is a common cause of children being "spoiled". Such children may unconsciously feel that they are not truly loved for who they are, but for what is expected from them. They may try to compensate for this lack of love in the only way they learned – by demanding more and more from parents and later from other people.

Many people believe that permissiveness alone creates spoiled children. Permissiveness is a part of the issue, but not the only one. Parents who lack healthy boundaries are unable to teach them to children. That presumes lack of self-esteem and mature love.

I read a newspaper article, which claimed that children become spoiled if parents give them "too much love". Too much (healthy) love is not possible. Too much unhealthy love is easily possible, if parents do not know how to care for themselves and set firm boundaries.

Some clients that I worked with, found it impossible to question the beliefs or behavior of their parents, because they feared that it would have meant ingratitude or selfishness. People who were conditioned by guilt, may not recognize that identifying mistakes in their upbringing does not mean ingratitude and disrespect. Recognizing and accepting parents as human beings, imperfect and limited by their past experiences, are signs of maturity.

Children can also become selfish if parents enforced discipline without respect or compassion. Such children can develop resistance to any responsibility, including reasonable and justified demands. They may start to be spiteful and disrespectful to others as soon as they are old enough to feel safe, or in environments where they feel more freedom than with their families.

Points to ponder:

Do you share your problems and unpleasant emotions with your child? Do you criticize the other parent to your child? Do you expect your child to understand and support you? Or do you need somebody to listen to you, adult or not?

Are you trying to earn or buy your child's love? Do you feel guilty if you take care of your own needs and say "no" to your child?

Practice:

If you feel lost or confused, consult an expert.

Avoid criticizing the other parent in front of children. Try to talk about the other parent with respect and understanding, even if (and especially if) you are in conflict or in the process of divorce. If you feel you have to talk about the other parent's unacceptable behavior, focus on the behavior and avoid criticizing his personality. In this way, you will avoid your children feeling rejected too.

Seek emotional support from your partner, parents or friends, not from children.

Fundamental Personality Splits

In this chapter, I will describe a process I notice in many families. If you do not recognize yourself in it, you probably had above-average parents. Either way, this chapter can help you to better understand other people's behavior.

Marina, an open and intelligent woman in her thirties, came to me because she wanted to improve her communication with and feelings about her mother. It soon became obvious that every time she would try to admit her own mistakes and recognize her mother's positive qualities, she would feel anger and resentment, followed by guilt and self-doubt. Her feelings for her mother were a constant inner conflict.

She described her mother as a reasonable woman who lived by her principles, but who was cold and demanding, expressing criticism much more often than acceptance. Marina discovered that she was unconsciously afraid that loving her mother also meant accepting her mother's criticisms towards her. This would trigger eruptions of anger.

Because of conditional love and unsupportive upbringing, some people learn to associate love with humiliation and power struggles. This is a reason for unconscious resistance to intimacy and difficulties opening up to other people.

Marina said that her mother mentioned similar experiences as a child, in which she may have learned to fear expressing love, even to her own daughter. Parents who are afraid that love might mean slavery, will be afraid to fully love even their own children, especially as children are demanding "by default". Thus parents might believe that it is their responsibility, or even their priority, to teach children that they cannot "always get their own way", even in situations when children's needs are natural and their wishes modest.

A parent might perceive natural childish (immature) behavior as wrong or unacceptable. For example, children naturally experiment with different role models and behaviors, forget their parents' requests and need time to develop compassion and unselfishness. Some parents do not understand that these are normal developmental stages and may label children as inherently "bad". That can result from one or more of the following:

- parents' immature expectations of perfection from other people, formed in their own childhoods. Expectation for children may be even higher, as many parents hope that their children will be "special"

- parents who project their feelings about their own parents onto their children (especially if the grandparents were immature and the parent felt responsible for them. For such people, any immature behavior may trigger memories of those experiences)

- parents with negative feelings about their own inner child and their own needs, feelings and desires (often created during experiences of continuous criticism in youth). Such parents might project this self-hatred onto children who remind them of their own unpleasant experiences.

Parents with such characteristics might consider themselves to be victims of their children if their expectations are not fulfilled. They might label their children spiteful and uncooperative. Such beliefs become further reinforced as the parent-child relationships worsen (which can be expected if the children are not too scared to resist).

Creation of inner conflict

For children, such labeling is a huge pressure. They might react with a conflict between love and blind trust on one side, and a strong wish to prove themselves on the other side. If you explore both of these feelings, you will probably describe them like this: either *they* (parents) are right and something is wrong with me; or *they* are wrong, they do not love me and they are being cruel – but why am I not loved? – in both cases, children conclude that they do not deserve to be loved.

According to Transactional Analysis, a child eventually adopts one of those two conclusions as a fixed idea, which leads to permanent "life positions": "+/-" (I am OK, they are not OK) or "-/+" (I am not OK, they are OK), and more rarely "-/-" (neither I nor they are OK) or "+/+" (a position which is desired and healthy; I am OK and they are also OK). In my opinion, such fixed positions (or masks) dominate the outer behavior, while under the surface inner conflict continues. In other words, overconfident people are likely to hide inferiority feelings, while insecure people might easily be hiding criticism to others.

In such ways, some children conclude that love is slavery. They may fear that if they show love, they will be manipulated, humiliated or shamed. This may be generalized to all life as an existential anxiety, especially in intimate relationships, and carried over to next generations.

With time, both parents and children in such situations start to avoid considering peaceful conversation or understanding, fearing that reconciliation might lead to more disappointment and humiliation. This can make it particularly difficult for people to admit their own faults and responsibility, because of strong emotions and the energy invested into blaming others. This helps avoid guilt and fears that something is wrong with them.

Childish parts often perceive the world as either black or white, and may feel that, in a conflict, only one person can be right – not both. Therefore, if we admit that we made a mistake, we are *bad*, which triggers not only feelings of guilt, shame and inadequacy, but also the idea that humiliation is a normal response to a mistake.

We cannot resolve such conflicts until we recognize and heal deeply suppressed beliefs that we are somehow bad, that we do not deserve love, and that we are less worthy than others. We easily create such beliefs at young ages, when other family members seem as big as trees and act so self-assured. (Immature parents often emphasize their positions of power by underestimating children, or by openly mocking them).

As long as these parts of us exist, related emotions will burst out from time to time, which also activates the other side of the inner conflict. Strong feelings of inadequacy usually provoke a need to defend ourselves, which often comes out as anger and spite. Trying to choose between one and the other is a mistake. If we try this, we cannot resolve the conflict because neither of those parts is our true self. In Soulwork, we resolve conflicts by exploring both parts, thus gradually approaching the original causes of such personality splits, which are usually covered up by a deep belief, "I cannot be me".

I find it logical that an imbalance or immature behavior has its counterbalance in an opposite tendency, which is suppressed. In other words, a person who, at first glance, gives up easily and appears weak, probably suppresses feelings of aggression and hostility, while aggressive people often suppress fear and insecurity.

The same process is triggered not only by parents (although that is usually the most obvious) but in other situations that remind us of the original problematic circumstances, even if the only similarity is the possibility that our opinions might be wrong.

All those internal processes are subtle, except in moments of crisis. Few people are aware of them because it is easier to avoid dealing with heavy emotions.

A child of immature parents may feel pushed into taking responsibility for them; this creates fear and feelings of inadequacy, followed by guilt and defensive anger. As children are likely to make black-and-white conclusions and generalizations, they might expand their negative attitudes towards other irrational acts of others, resulting in unhealthy moralizing. Empty intellectualism is one possibility – escaping from feelings into thoughts. Such people often perceive expressions of feelings as weak and immature. The opposite extreme is delinquency – acts of spiteful children, who avoid responsibility and justify their behavior with perceived unfairness of others.

When describing these situations, I do not suggest you search for who to blame, rather to develop your empathy and understanding of yourself and others. If you want to resolve a problem, you first need to admit and accept it.

Points to ponder:

If you are a parent, can you accept that your children will sometimes express demanding and immature behavior? How do you feel in such situations?

Can you accept your family and open up to them? Are you afraid that their demands might suffocate you or their behavior might irritate you? Does anything stop you setting boundaries?

Practice:

Whenever you find yourself angry or in conflict with someone, check if you have conflicting feelings inside.

Explore any resistance to accept people as they are.

Attention Deficit Disorder and Hyperactivity

More and more children are being labeled with ADD and ADHD diagnoses, yet hardly anyone seems to have a clear idea about what those terms actually mean. Attention deficit disorder and hyperactivity are often defined by how a child behaves in school, focusing on behavior that violates school rules and on fulfilling obligations such as homework and self-study.

It is still too seldom discussed, to what extent school rules and demands are natural and adjusted to children. Is it appropriate to put a six year old into a concrete box with 20-30 other children and expect that they all sit still and listen to (often not very interesting) lectures for several hours each day? This is only possible in an educational system in which obedience is rewarded and creativity discouraged.

Nowadays in the West, relationships and communication are less and less restricted. As children observe different models of behavior in different media (sometimes models of individuality and unconventionality, but more often of aggression and immaturity), conflicts between school rules and media input increase. This creates inner conflicts in children, which are rarely relieved, considering that few schoolchildren receive sufficient attention or adult support.

Yet attention deficit disorders are not only natural responses of children to boring conditions. Other elements also contribute to children showing signs of distraction, impulsiveness or restlessness, and not just in school.

Television, computers and video games are now hugely influential, and their contents are becoming much faster, frenetic and very often aggressive. The more time children spend in front of televisions or playing video games, the more they become accustomed to strong stimuli and impulsive action, that lack real world consequences.

In the real world, the stimuli are more often gentle, slower paced - and reactions have consequences. Children may feel bored; their nerve systems accustomed to intense excitement, they seek more and stronger stimuli. Similarly, when we get used to a specific taste, (e.g. chili) we might want it even stronger, and we may miss it if we have to do without it.

According to Jerry Mander, television triggers strong feelings and needs for action, while forcing passivity and suppression of those urges. In this way, nervous and muscle tension accumulate that cannot be expressed while a child is focused on a TV show. After the show is over, it can be difficult for children to express and release that energy and tension in constructive ways.

If you have played computer or video games, you may have noticed similar restlessness in yourself, tension and search for outer stimuli. If you are used to an active and dynamic job and suddenly you take an inactive vacation or sick leave, you may feel restless and useless. People who retire from management jobs, without other work to do, might try to spend their time managing their families (who may not appreciate this blessing).

In my opinion, a balance between periods of external activity and periods of introspection is ideal. We can get to know ourselves better and learn to find stimulation in our internal worlds. If we learn to think creatively, outside our usual limits, this can be a source of enthusiasm and fun. This makes boredom impossible, as opposed to constantly reviewing recurring, similar thoughts. Creative thinking requires time and practice, however.

Sensory sensitivities

Attention deficit disorders may also reflect children's individual sensitivities, as described by Dr. Stanley Greenspan in his book "The Challenging Child". He emphasizes that different children (and adults) have different sensitivities to specific sensory stimuli. For example, if children are "extra sensitive" to auditory stimuli, small environmental sounds can disturb their concentration (for example, fleas feeding on a cat might sound like vacuum cleaners). If children are "insufficiently" sensitive to sounds, a teacher's voice may not attract and keep their attention. A man told me that his son complained that his computer was "too loud". "How can a computer possibly be too loud?" asked the father, suspecting a plot to get a new computer. For children sensitive to sounds, it may well be. This also applies to visual, olfactory and tactile stimuli.

Some children are particularly receptive to sensory information that are neglected in schools. Most lectures focus on audio information, i.e. words, spoken or written. This could work well for auditory sensitive children, but many children learn better in other ways, e.g. visual stimuli, personal experience, activities etc. Our schools too often neglect these kinds of stimuli; it may offer some in the first years of primary school, but little thereafter.

Such individual differences may not cause hyperactivity and attention deficit disorder by themselves. ADD can develop if children's individual needs are not recognized, if the children are labeled as problematic or punished. While Dr. Greenspan mostly focuses on children's sensory sensibilities and genetically determined characteristics, his descriptions of parents who bring children to him indicate that these parents are often tense, impatient, insecure or controlling. They may misinterpret the child's behavior and rarely spend enough quality time with their children.

With such family backgrounds, some children who could otherwise adjust to societal rules, develop unpleasant self-images that motivate maladjusted behaviors.

From my point of view, sensory sensitivity and even the influence of television and video games are secondary causes of attention deficit disorder. I believe that the foundation of this problem is often a child's need to escape his own unpleasant feelings. This can happen if a child does not get enough love and understanding, if important people express unresolved tensions such as anxiety or anger, or if parents are in a long-term conflict.

Some adults cannot stand silence and inactivity - they avoid experiencing their own feelings, for example anxiety, depression or guilt. They might keep a TV or a radio (or both) constantly ON, compulsively avoid solitude or may be highly active in Internet forums and social networks.

In similar ways, some children distract themselves from their emotions. They direct their attention externally, shifting from one stimulus to another, which keeps their minds busy. But they cannot stay focused on one thing, the stimuli have to change. The longer they focus on the same stimulus, the more automatically their minds process it. More and more attention is available to be directed within.

For example, if you can drive a car (or play a musical instrument) so well that it becomes a routine, you may find yourself more occupied with your thoughts and feelings than with driving or playing. To keep your attention outside, you need changing stimuli.

For some people, a television or a radio in the background is enough to occupy their "extra" attention, leaving no space for noticing suppressed emotions. However, stressed children are more likely to become addicted to video games (and later, perhaps to other addictions), than emotionally stable children that are not overly burdened with unpleasant feelings.

Dr. Greenspan described a girl with attention deficit disorder, who once lucidly summarized her distracted, scattered activity as a way to make external stress – schoolwork, dissatisfied parents, criticisms and expectations – disappear for a while. Shifting attention to outer stimuli enabled her to forget about her external burdens as well as her feelings of inadequacy. Of course, this would cause even more criticism, pressure and accumulation of obligations and the vicious circle would continue.

It is not surprising that Greenspan's primary approach to treating ADD children was to increase quality time with their parents, while teaching parents to recognize unique qualities and needs of their children. With this approach, children can feel safe while exploring different ways to relate to the world.

Children Need Challenges

We notice that people from problematic, chaotic families often develop important resources early. For example: intelligence (in order to understand confusing situations and to find way out of them), perseverance, inner strength, ability to cope with difficulties, sensitivity, empathy, sense of humor (as a way of relieving one's own and other people's unpleasant emotions, or as a strategy to find one's place within a group).

Likewise, we frequently notice that children who grow up in protective families that provide everything, often do not become particularly strong or motivated people. Sometimes they can become egotistic and spoiled, especially in the last several decades of the 20th century. Since "children first" has become a prevalent attitude, many parents seem to neglect setting boundaries and teaching children to cooperate with others. (This unbalanced attitude might be a reaction to the "adults first" approach of past centuries - and family health requires balancing everybody's needs.)

Every family is a complex whole, and a child's experiences are "multidimensional". A certain influence can cause several different consequences. Some may be unpleasant, while others can be useful and important. Chaos and trauma can motivate people to develop important resources and qualities as a way to survive. On the other hand, such circumstances can also cause fear, anger, guilt and a poor self-image. Parental care and attention can create a feeling that we are worthy and acceptable – yet if challenges are lacking, we might develop average or below average abilities, lack of motivation and low self-confidence. As in the case of most circumstances, consequences are rarely black and white, but usually a combination of "positive" and "negative".

Some people who were strongly protected by their parents, claim that this very protection made them insecure and unable to cope with life challenges. They did not learn how to cope with unpleasant situations, or to practice resourcefulness and creativity. On the other hand, few people would prefer to have suffered neglect, abuse or ridicule. People who were neglected as children know very well the high price paid for their inner strength, such as unpleasant emotional baggage.

Does this mean you have to neglect or traumatize your children so that they become resourceful? No. With some awareness and effort, you can make it possible for your children to "have their cake and eat it too". What is important are not strong or frequent unpleasant experiences, rather significant and frequent challenges. Families who protect their children may neglect the children's need to face challenging situations, which would stimulate their resources.

Shaping challenges

You can shape challenges so that they stimulate thinking, perception, sensitivity and strength, while simultaneously being caring and attentive to your child. The key is in giving your children emotional support, while encouraging them to complete as many challenging tasks as possible.

Adjust the challenges to the stage of children's development. Target approximately the upper limit of their current abilities, exceeding just a little beyond their "comfort zones". Choose tasks that are demanding, but not so difficult for children to feel discouraged and start doubting themselves.

Children do this spontaneously, always reaching a little higher, always trying to get a little further and better. Observe your children carefully to find out if a challenge suits them. If a child is at least partially interested and motivated, continue. If you notice strong signs of stress or fear, it may be a good idea to postpone the task and find an easier one.

Provide as many different challenges as possible. Provide physical tasks (dressing, tying shoelaces), include children in household work (but do not give them your best china to wash) and set intellectual tasks (e.g. acquire books of puzzles or games that require thinking). Teach a child to read or to speak a foreign language as early as possible. Most two or three-year old children can slowly start recognizing letters, and by the age of four, many children are ready to start reading. Include social tasks (set relationship and communication related goals). Shape challenges as games, as often as possible.

Avoid offering ready-made solutions to the child. Instead, help children consider possible solutions by asking additional questions. For example, encourage them to create as many solutions as possible, e.g. "Johnny is ridiculed by other children at school. Think of ten different things that Johnny could do about it!" Follow children's thinking and help them with questions such as: "What could go wrong? Who else could you include? What is important to know about those children? Why do they behave like that? Have you forgotten something? Can some of these solutions be improved?" Be gentle with your questions and do not push so much to the point of discouraging the child.

Certainly, lack of time is a problem for many parents. However, you do not have to sit with your children all day asking them such questions. You can have such conversations during normal daily occurrences. Take advantage of situations when your child has a real problem (there will be enough of those!). You can use whatever opportunities become available to think about new challenges for your child.

While avoiding risk of serious injury, let your children occasionally get hurt, scratched or burned, if they ignore your warnings. This will not have emotional consequences, and children learn reasonable caution and to better assess their abilities and the consequences of their actions. Avoid attempting - except in extreme situations- to solve their conflicts with other children. Let them do it. Children can cope with the unpleasantness of these conflicts quite successfully, if they have your emotional support and encouragement.

Many people experience more social challenges as children than as adults. You can help children evaluate such conflicts and possible solutions. If your children fight amongst themselves, intervene if necessary, but avoid random punishments. Help children discuss how they feel and what they want. You might need to protect one child if the other is older or a persistent bully, while considering what motivates the latter to be violent.

Avoid trying to make daily tasks too easy for your children. As soon as they can do something- eat, dress up, go to school alone- avoid doing it for them, as much as possible. Doing things together makes tasks less boring, improves your relationship and gives you time to talk. Emotional support and acceptance are particularly important. Avoid verbal or non-verbal criticism, give accurate feedback when needed. Avoid undeserved praise, but let children know when you appreciate their efforts and results. You will make your children's and your own lives more fulfilling, both short term and long term.

In these ways, by applying focused effort and awareness, you can help your children build firm foundations, strong stepping-stones for creating high quality lives.

Gender Equality

A society that oppresses women digs its own grave, since mostly women raise the next generation. Unhappy women with low self-esteem cannot teach their children to be happy and loving. All other cultural differences are just details.

We can observe around the world that societies in which women are respected are also the happiest and most advanced. By "advanced" I do not necessarily mean technological and economical opportunities (even if some connections can be made), but primarily emotional and social quality of life (for example in Scandinavian countries). When societies humiliate women in subtle ways (such as lower pay for equal skills, or presenting them as sexual objects), there are consequences too.

However, women share responsibility for a change. In my experience, women criticize men more openly than the other way around, and most men I know praise women more than they praise men. However, perhaps my work does not attract average and below-average men, and if I had more contact with them, I would have a different impression.

Anyway, criticizing men is a victim behavior, and rarely constructive. It is unrealistic to expect immature men to grow up quickly; their disrespect for women is based on their early experiences of their parents' behavior. Boys raised in *macho* societies may feel relieved when they become aware that they are not girls. They try to act as manly as possible to "deserve" the freedom and respect they see adult men getting and to avoid their sisters' treatment. Their societies force them to prove their "manhood", and humiliate or reject them if they show any "feminine" behaviors. Their mothers and sisters may support this as much as fathers and brothers.

Some mothers encourage their daughters (and sisters, daughters in law, etc.) less than their sons. They expect less from daughters and appreciate them less. Unconsciously, this reflects the same disrespect that such women feel for themselves.

A mother has much more influence than a father in shaping a child's basic self-image and perception of the world. The younger the child, the deeper and more influential these impressions, and in the first few years, a mother is usually much closer. (The pre-natal period is probably just as important.)

When working with clients, I find that people whose mothers were less emotionally mature than their fathers, usually find it more difficult to change their habits and beliefs. A father definitely influences a child's personality, beliefs and emotional habits (which might cause problems later in life) but still influences the deepest, most basic self-image less than a mother.

Taking responsibility means making ourselves happy first, providing a respectful atmosphere for our children of either sex, and avoiding whatever supports prejudice (for example sending little girls to beauty contests).

Such changes cannot be aggressively imposed on others. A woman needs to be gentle, but persistent. Societal change is best achieved by women using their own behavior as examples. People (especially children) learn mostly by observing others' actions and consequences.

Words by themselves, especially critical words, rarely have any useful effect.

Points to ponder:

Are you inclined to trust male or female authorities more? (For example in commercials that show men or women as authorities.)

If you have children, does their gender change how you perceive their skills and abilities? What were your expectations during pregnancy or when the children were just born, according to expected gender of the child?

If you plan to have children, do you hope for a particular gender? If so, why?

Are you happy in your marriage and your other relationships? Do you tolerate patronizing or chauvinistic behavior, whether directed at yourself or the women around you?

What kind of an example do you set for your children?

Practice:

Observe your attitudes and comments concerning gender.

Avoid buying from companies that use gender prejudices in their marketing. (e.g. a commercial showing a man who "travels a lot and is very experienced" and his wife who "never traveled, but trusts her husband" and looks at him with admiration.)

Practice calm resistance in situations where someone is belittled based on gender.

Everybody Has a Story

When adults communicate with children, they may not see them as complete human beings, but more as something to manipulate. Most people repeat the child-raising methods used by their own parents. Parents, especially when in challenging situations, are likely to repeat these old habits, whether due to lack of time, patience or, most often, awareness.

I once observed a neighboring family with three daughters, of which one was three years old – the age in which socialization is most intense. While I was there, hardly a minute passed without at least three criticisms or mocking comments directed towards the little girl by her mother or her older sister. She was criticized because she did not remember some words or names, because she could not properly pronounce some words, because she could not draw as well as older children... The little girl was confused and oscillated between showing hurt, shame or anger. Her mother and sister would notice her state just enough to laugh at her. (I have to mention that the mother's tone of voice was mostly kind, even in criticism, which makes this situation better than what I have seen in some other families). If you add the father to this story, other older members of the family, neighbors, teachers... I felt deep compassion for that little girl, knowing that this will continue for the rest of the day, and in the next days, weeks and years.

This is an example of how many families treat children. In some families, the situation is even worse: I sometimes heard curses, threats and blaming directed to even the smallest children. Sometimes I am truly in awe of the strong foundations of our nature. Even after so much criticism, scorn and unrealistic demands, most of us grow up to become relatively stable and more or less willing to love. When I listen to the stories of my clients, again and again I admire the strength of human beings to overcome such tough circumstances.

However, most of us end up with many emotional issues that we carefully hide from others, even from ourselves. If a certain situation triggers suppressed emotions or compulsive urges, it is very difficult to look at it objectively and to act with respect towards everyone involved. Then we can act out our childish emotions. External observers might find it difficult to understand, but easy to judge such behavior. On the other hand, these same observers so full of judgments, in situations when their own strong emotions are triggered, will easily justify their own immature behavior.

There is a saying, "You cannot understand another person unless you walk a few miles in his shoes". Our strong emotions trigger an inner dialogue in which we convince ourselves that our perception and experience is the only correct interpretation. We might be rationally aware of our overreacting to details, yet the emotions are so strong that despite common sense we convince ourselves of the other person's bad or wrong intentions. After our emotions calm down, we might feel ashamed of our behavior, but while we are overwhelmed by childish emotions, it is very difficult to achieve such detachment.

Immature behavior of one person can trigger immature reactions from other people. While we are immersed in infantile emotions (often called age regression), it may feel humiliating even to consider the others' perspective (not to mention to admit mistakes and apologize), and we may justify our own aggression.

Many people expect others to be responsible, mature, considerate or show socially accepted behavior in every situation. If others do not fully meet our expectations, we may enjoy mentally judging them or discussing them with friends. Noticing other people's faults can be a welcome relief from (often unconscious) lack of self-esteem. Meanwhile, we rarely consider the others' past, their emotional conditioning, pain and defense mechanisms, inner needs and battles. At the same time, we may avoid communicating directly and truthfully to the person whose behavior we dislike, due to our own limitations (often things that we dislike in others).

Similarly, we may perceive any immature and careless behaviors of others as personal insults and direct rudeness, which is often not true. Often we focus on behavioral details and use them to judge the whole person. We may forget that everyone has their own history, a whole lifetime of experiences, beliefs, emotions (often painful ones). The resulting behavior is often not directed at us at all.

At the same time, we may feel an urge to justify our own compulsive behavior, as well as an urge to criticize others. Unfortunately, we may act in this way towards children, seeing details in their behavior as personality faults. In this way, we teach children to be judgmental and critical of themselves and others.

Points to ponder:

Do you expect mature and perfect behavior from others?

Do you feel an urge to criticize and judge others? Explore that urge. What feelings do you find? What is it that you truly need?

Practice:

In which situations do you have difficulty controlling your emotions, even if you know that they are not appropriate? If needed, use the "Exploring Emotions" process in the appendix of this book.

Notice when you share your criticisms of someone with your friends. How do you feel if you try to resist this urge?

When communicating to others, especially to children whose behavior is upsetting you, practice describing their behavior without judging their personality. Talk about yourself, your needs and desires. Particularly avoid attributing negative characteristics and intentions onto others.

Try to understand other people's feelings and perceptions. Then check how your perspective of a problematic situation changes.

Love and Partnership

Do you enjoy loving your intimate partner? Contrary to their hopes, many people find *love* to be a source of pain rather than bliss. There is no other adult relationship in which the depth and strength of our needs, imprints and beliefs from childhood become so obvious and strong, so persistent and overwhelming. Our emotions and hopes often resist both willpower and rational perspectives.

It is useful to understand that much of what we call loving feelings is our deepest, earliest memories coming to the surface, including unresolved inner conflicts. We go through our lives constantly seeking resolution for those conflicts, even if unconsciously.

I particularly enjoy working with clients' partnership issues. In other areas of life, in which we are usually more objective, dissociated and less emotionally involved, we do not become so aware of our deep emotional patterns. Partnership issues reflect our deepest emotions and most fundamental beliefs, and if resolved, allow beautiful changes that encourage your health and well-being, as well as the health of your children.

Building attraction

If you are in love with someone, do people who remind you of that person attract your attention and evoke your emotions? In my opinion, the same process happens when noticing potential intimate partners, except that we are unconsciously reminded of parents. Our minds spontaneously search for associations, and we unconsciously seek people with characteristics that we have learned to associate with love.

A potential partner does not need to be strikingly similar to a parent for emotional attraction to occur. Usually, there are a few essential characteristics — for example, the person's emotional maturity, communication habits and ability to give and receive love.

Remember your feelings when you were in love: were they dominantly childish or mature? Falling in love usually triggers a kaleidoscope of immature emotions. Did you feel euphoria and unrealistically idealized the other person when things were well? Perhaps you were almost obsessed and overly sensitive to details in the loved one's behavior. Most people experience childlike, exaggerated unpleasant emotions when reality does not fulfill their expectations. I often ask myself, does anyone actually know what true love is?

I remember an experience that gave me a clear insight about the mechanism of falling in love. I was in a group of people and became emotionally engaged in a discussion. While most people opposed my opinion, a man expressed unexpected support and understanding for my point of view. In that instant, I felt attracted to him. This progressed in the days that followed, in spite of my awareness that the man had many traits I disliked and that it would be extremely difficult to create a quality relationship with him.

I looked into myself and found an insecure infantile part of me, to which his support was like rain in a desert. My "inner child" started to feel intense hope that I could get the understanding, acceptance and support I had always wished for. I started attributing many positive qualities to this man, hoping that he truly possessed them. At the same time, I ignored or justified the immature aspects of his behavior, instead worrying about how I would appear in his eyes.

When I healed my childish beliefs about myself, and loved and supported my inner child, my infatuation dissolved. I doubt I would have had such success if I had tried to force myself to fall out of love.

It is illusory to hope that we can create healthy, mature partnerships without resolving our emotional patterns. They will not resolve themselves on their own. Many of our patterns are deeply unconscious and difficult to recognize, and many are presented globally as expressions of love. Jealousy, obsession, taking responsibility for the other person's feelings, suffering when the other person does not fulfill our needs ... all these are presented in media as proofs of love.

When I think about myself and my clients, I notice that we are usually attracted to people who have both positive and negative qualities similar to important members of our primary families. If your parents were mature in certain situations and areas of life, and expressed mature love, you could have learned that this was normal, and you are not likely to be attracted to people who show immature behavior in those situations. On the other hand, if you learned to perceive immature behavior of your parents as normal, your life may reflect unfulfilled needs and you may adopt similar behavior style.

Are you confused and angry because you attract complicated relationships? Consider if you would tolerate easy, relaxed relationships. Would you even be attracted to a person with whom you might have a peaceful and happy partnership? Many people only feel safe and "at home" in immature relationships.

Explore your feelings if you are attracted to somebody while rationally knowing that it would not be wise to start a partnership with that person. What is particularly attractive to you? It could be certain facial expressions, posture, or some other details of that person's behavior. How old appears to be the part of you that is attracted? What does that part of you hope to receive or achieve through that relationship?

Physical attributes are important to many people, especially teenagers. Yet, as we grow older, attractive bodies may not be enough. We might notice people with good-looking bodies, but it takes much more to fall in love. That "more", which we may not notice consciously, are often tiny non-verbal signals that correspond to what is familiar from childhood.

Is falling in love a curse or a blessing? To people who keep creating unhealthy relationships, it might seem a curse. On the other hand, a partnership is a powerful way to become aware of subconscious patterns that need to be resolved. If you are ready and if you take responsibility, partnership can be a springboard to fast improvement.

Patterns in Intimate Relationships

Perhaps you can recognize particular types of personality and behaviors that you feel attracted to, even if they are problematic. Appearances and behavior may not be obviously similar amongst your different partners throughout your life, but you may recognize patterns in how you felt about those people, and in how your relationships developed.

In the experience that we call love (or, more precisely, infatuation), our healthy enthusiasm and appreciation of other people is often mixed with transferences and bonds. There are **three common types of unhealthy bonds**.

First, our subconscious hopes and needs from childhood can make us prone to idealize certain people, just as we idealized our parents when we were small children. We wanted happy, warm relationships in which we could feel secure, protected and valuable. Remember the hope and elation in the first stages of infatuation; irrational feeling that you have finally found someone who can fulfill your deepest needs and make you feel accepted, loved and valuable. If you explore which details of the appearance and behavior of this person trigger your emotions, you might recognize a pattern and perhaps connect it to memories from your early years.

The second way of bonding is trying to heal our toxic, painful beliefs about ourselves, through (hopefully) earning love in similar circumstances in which those beliefs were created. Unconsciously, we may be attracted to a similar type of environment that our parents created in our first family, the consequences of which were never completely resolved within our subconscious. The child in us still hopes to resolve confusions and inner conflicts from the past, searching for people to love who would compensate for our parent(s).

In our earliest years, we judged ourselves according to reactions of our environment. Children are sensitive to non-verbal signals from their parents, to how parents express their feelings for them. They try to understand and adapt to what is acceptable and expected, even if it is painful and confusing. This is how we may often feel in love relationships.

You can see many people who are otherwise smart, confident and able to recognize unhealthy behavior, suddenly become aware of their every word or move and anxiously try to anticipate the feelings and expectations of a specific other person. They may feel as if their value, fulfillment and future happiness depend on a person who they don't even know well.

Remember the feelings of confusion, pain and reviewing your behavior because of some detail your beloved said or did. Those experiences may give you an idea about how you felt as a child in relation to your parents. I am not saying that children feel like that all the time - sometimes children are more sensitive than at other times. Keep in mind that all of your emotions have a source, and that the sources of many irrational emotions are in our earliest years of life.

Few people recognize or remember how sensitive they were to their parents' behavior, how dependent on them, how much they needed parental love, approval and acceptance. These feelings are normally long forgotten, because they happened at an age in which individual identity, conscious memory and awareness, not to mention rational thinking, were undeveloped.

The more we grow up, the more realistic is our perception of the world (hopefully). We are less likely to be overwhelmed with exaggerated hopes and expectations in adulthood than in childhood or adolescence. Still, in the right circumstances, with a combination of the right triggers by one person, the child parts of us wake up quickly and even mature people can find themselves overwhelmed with long forgotten emotions.

The third type of bond is being attracted to behaviors and emotions that we learned to accept as normal and even loving in our early family, even if painful. The most obvious examples are abusive relationships. People who repeatedly find themselves in abusive relationships, often told me that they perceived healthy people and relationships as not passionate, not loving enough, or even boring. It comes down to what we feel is normal.

Some children might recognize at quite an early age that violence is not a strange way to love and cannot be justified with the child's behavior. This understanding depends on their constitution and temper, and on their families. Often, they were surrounded with ongoing and uncontrolled violence and injustice, but still had some other people around who were models of healthy and loving behavior, perhaps a grandfather, sister, aunt or even a neighbor. With their help, such children could still learn to distinguish between love and violence.

Such a person might search for a partner with a determination to find someone who is healthier and more mature than the parent(s). Sometimes they can be successful. Still, patterns created before these children developed a realistic perspective, or even felt separate from parents, will continue, maybe expressed in subtle ways.

Cheri grew up in an unhealthy family, but she made a strong decision to choose a partner different than her aggressive, manipulative and narrow-minded father. She chose a man who appeared calm, gentle, responsible and thoughtful. But after years of marriage, when their relationship settled into a routine, it became more and more apparent that the gentle and sensitive appearance of her husband was hiding a cluster of suppressed emotions based on deep guilt and shame from his childhood.

Her husband slowly became more and more emotionally withdrawn, unable to enjoy intimacy or clear communication, while showing passive aggression in situations of conflict or misunderstanding. So Cheri, even if she recognized and avoided an openly abusive relationship, eventually admitted to herself that she was participating in a relationship that reflected her childhood feelings of loneliness and rejection.

Like Cheri, many people have told me that they could not recognize the character similarities between their partners and their parents, neither in the beginning of the relationship, nor during the first few years. Some people can control and suppress their unhealthy patterns for a long time... until routine and everyday stress lead to careless communication and taking each other for granted. Once those patterns have emerged, we can, almost without exception, recognize behaviors that hurt us since childhood.

"My parents spoiled me and gave me everything I wanted. I can't possibly see how my (painful and abusive) partnership could have anything to do with them. (...) I remember saying to my partner, "The only people who ever hurt me so much were you and my father!" (quote from a client)

It seems that we are all deeply sensitive to almost invisible signals that trigger feelings of familiarity and intimacy ... even if the more obvious signals seem to indicate the opposite. This is probably why, out of many people we meet, only rarely will someone trigger intense infatuation.

It is very rare that we meet potential partners who have the qualities that we consciously desire AND who express the tiny and almost invisible non-verbal signals that we unconsciously seek. Such signals trigger hopes that our deepest longings can finally be fulfilled ... and, eventually, bring our painful memories to the surface. Such a combination creates the most powerful infatuation and obsession with the other person.

There are three basic ways in which we create emotional patterns and beliefs that shape our relationships:

1. **Personal experience with parents**: whether our parents treated us with love and healthy appreciation, or in a controlling, humiliating and aggressive manner, their behavior became natural to us. Unconsciously, we probably associated it with love and started to expect it. As small children, we also created fixed ideas that we deserved such behavior. If a parent acted like a needy, dependent victim (e.g. addicted), we might have developed a deep urge to help - and thus deserve love. In that case, as adults, we may still be attracted to people who appear to need help and sympathy. A big part of our intimate relationships might be described as subliminal attempts to earn love in circumstances similar to when we needed it most - in our early childhood.

2. **Modeling and identifying** with parents' behavior. Children learn through identifying with parents, taking over their gender roles, behavior, beliefs and prejudice. This becomes particularly obvious in our intimate relationships.

3. **Relationship between parents**. How parents communicated to each other - their words and idioms, the way they shared (or avoided) work and responsibilities ... the younger we were, the more likely we accepted it as normal. During misunderstandings and conflicts with our partners, it is easy to automatically repeat our parents' behavior. In such a way, we can create an atmosphere similar to our early family. We might be so convinced it's normal, that we might not question or analyze our behavior.

A common example of a complementary pattern would be an emotionally closed, cold man and an emotionally hungry, demanding woman. Such behaviors are partly based on gender differences, but more on unhealthy family histories. Most commonly, such closed men grew up with pushy or needy mothers, whether they were controlling their sons or pretending to be victims. Their sons developed coldness and withdrawal as defense, perhaps imitating their fathers. Sometimes both parents might be pushy, or their roles might be reversed.

A needy woman was most likely ignored by one or both parents, often but not always her father. Trying to win his attention, she learned to use different approaches: trying to please him, crying, anger, complaints, perhaps manipulation and playing victim - whatever worked best or whatever she observed from her mother, for example.

A withdrawn, distant partner will trigger her father-related memories and emotions: feeling abandoned, neglected or unworthy. She will then automatically try to use her childish reactions, first in mild, then in more intense ways. Her behavior triggers her partner's memories: he may feel that his boundaries are threatened, or that he is being used and manipulated and has nowhere to hide ... except within (or within a bar). Add to that low quality communication by both partners, also learned in their families, and that leads to vicious circles that create more and more stress, disappointment, anger and resentment. At the same time, such partners may both hope that the other will change, while being unwilling to change themselves. They might feel trapped, while simultaneously fearing the loss of their relationship and a chance to heal their childhood trauma.

Unfortunately, most couples start looking for help only after their mutual trust is deeply damaged and their motivation is almost exhausted. Even tiny details in one partner's behavior remind the other partner of past frustrations and resentments. It might be very difficult for such a couple to start again; to practice noticing and correcting unhealthy emotions and communication together. They may lack the patience to allow each other to occasionally repeat old mistakes, while learning to communicate in new, unfamiliar ways.

More examples of bonding based on childish emotions:

1. A woman attracted to a domineering, controlling man, who she perceives as strong, decisive and confident, just as she perceived her father who acted in a similar manner. As she did as a child, she hopes that she will win and "earn" his attention and approval, and is bonded by that hope. Perhaps the man's mother was childish or weak, so the son learned

to perceive all women in this way, probably following his father's beliefs. At the same time, he might feel deep attraction based on an unconscious hope that his partner will change in the way his mother did not, by taking responsibility for herself, becoming stronger and giving him the kind of love and approval he longed for.

2. A woman who is attracted to ambivalent, unpredictable men who act gentle and warm in one moment, and aggressive and arrogant in the next. Their unpleasant behaviors remind her of her childish feeling of not being worthy. Then she longs even more for the comfort and support she feels in the moments of the man's pleasant and warm behavior. Such men are likely to carry deep inner conflicts between different parts of their personalities. For example, his healthy, warm feelings may well conflict with his anger and resentment for his parents; or perhaps he felt that he had to act one role in front of father, and another in front of mother. Such conflicts cannot be resolved by rationalizing, willpower or even by the love of a partner.

3. A man full of guilt and self-doubt, who enters a relationship or even marriage mostly to avoid hurting a woman. Of course, such behavior makes him feel even more bonded to her by guilt and suppressed resentment, instead of by love. He might hope for resolution and forgiveness. He might fall in love with another woman, who will trigger his hopes of love and bliss, but will feel too guilty to leave his current partner. His partner might be controlling and manipulative, out of an early childish conclusion that she cannot earn or be given love, but has to control people to receive at least some kind of attention.

Everybody who ever fell in love had a chance to experience to what extent emotions from childhood are deep and overwhelming, to what extent they evade all rational arguments and decisions. If you are in such a relationship now, you have a perfect chance to recognize how you felt as a child and what you still carry within. A chance, also, to change those feelings, primarily through healing your inner child, exercising self-love and learning quality communication.

Assuming that you are not abused, it might be better not to force yourself to end such a relationship if you feel it would be emotionally difficult. If you end your relationship without resolving your emotional patterns first, you will probably repeat similar patterns in your future relationships. Instead, focus on working with your childhood emotions, until you feel less and less attracted to your unhealthy partner. Then you can end the relationship without strong emotions and inner conflict. Or perhaps you will notice that, the more healthy and mature your behavior becomes, the more your partner will change in a similar way. This is an indication that your emotions were a consequence of transference, not reality.

To stay in a relationship or not to stay?

Most people, at some point in their lives, experience a "should I stay or should I go" conflict. This is common if we are in a relationship that is not truly satisfying, but in which we do receive some love (or we hope we would in future). Even people who otherwise have no problems making decisions, can find themselves struggling with this one.

When we are in love, we hope that our partners love us, even if their behavior shows rejection and immaturity. I see it as childish hope, a reflection of hope that our parents loved us after all. As children, we attempted to perceive our parents' behavior as loving, in any way possible. If it was not possible, the next defense was to ignore it. To children, a realization that parents were unable or unwilling to love them would be too frightening. As adults, we create similar situations, but now those childish parts of us may be deeply suppressed and unconscious.

What would convince you that someone really loves you? In the same way that you try to evaluate someone's honesty, no matter what type of relationship you are in, you should pay more attention to their behavior than to their words. "Words are cheap" and saying nice things is easy, especially if one has a good idea of what the other person wants to hear. Many people, however, when they are in love, ignore what they see and cling to nice words to feed their hope.

To make things more complicated, perhaps the other person truly believes he or she is sincere and loving. People who abuse or intimidate their partners, often believe that they love them and that such behavior is normal. The abused people also want to believe they are loved. Only after they end such a relationship and look back on it, can they understand some aspects of the partners' behavior that they failed to see before. Such people often repeat their early childhood conditioning.

Imagine looking at a person whom you love, or at a potential partner, as if you were watching a TV program with no sound: as if you could see only movements, facial expressions and actions. How would this behavior appear if someone else were involved and not you? Maybe you would recognize lack of respect and consideration, or immaturity and fear of intimacy? Perhaps it would not be something that would make you end the relationship (there is no point in searching for perfection in anyone) but in your infatuation, you avoided noticing that you felt hurt. How much better could your relationship be if you both work on it?

When we are in love, it is very difficult to be completely honest with ourselves. We bond to our partner and our relationship with a similar blind intensity and need with which we trusted our parents and needed their love. This is most obvious when we have to decide whether to end a relationship which obviously does not fulfill our needs, even though we still feel romantic attraction. Whilst the relationship is stable, we usually believe that we are aware of our partner's faults and that we react to them maturely enough. When a problem arises that could endanger the relationship, we begin to search for ways to justify and minimize the significance of the problem.

We may use myths to justify our inner conflict. A common myth is that true love does not ask for anything in return; that is, we may expect ourselves to love the other person unconditionally and ignore unwanted behaviors. Some people, blinded by this idea, stay in unhappy relationships and try to be satisfied with their own love alone. Sooner or later, they learn that it is essential to take care of their own feelings, and that it takes two for a healthy relationship. We cannot experience partnership love, intimacy and companionship on our own, we can only experience them in a relationship with a compatible person. If we stay in relationships with immature people, we deprive ourselves of the possibility to experience the full potential of a healthy mutual love.

Most people are still in the process of learning how to take care of themselves and how to find balance between their own needs and the needs of others. Sometimes it means discovering what we truly want and what we cannot settle for, no matter what. Unconditional love is a nice concept – if it does not include neglecting yourself. Also, unconditional love is the attitude of a parent to a child – and you probably do not want such kind of relationship with your partner.

A key issue is how we define "love". To change the type of relationship – for example to give up the partnership and become just friends – does not necessarily mean that we would stop loving that person. It is more likely that we could love him or her even more, if we stop expecting something that that person cannot give us.

The point is not in demanding something from a specific person, but to know what we want in a specific relationship type and to be aware of our needs. If this means changing the relationship type, it does not mean that we need to feel disappointed and angry. Actually, it is healthier to end an incompatible relationship before the buildup of anger and resentment. Then we can move on to seek personal fulfillment, instead of leaving somebody because of his or her faults. We need emotional independence to do that, which is not easy to achieve.

Neale Donald Walsh wrote: "*The purpose of a relationship is not to find the other one who will fulfill you, but to have the other with whom you can share your fullness*". How much sense does it make to stay in a relationship because of "love", if we cannot achieve the above? Love is so rarely the true motivation. Much more often, we are motivated by unhealthy bonding, self-deceit and hope that the other person would change.

Many people try to change their partners, sometimes staying in a relationship (or returning after a break-up) because they see their partners' potential and hope that they would become motivated to fulfill it and change for the better. This is often an illusion. There are a relatively small number of people who feel strong inner motivation to change, and even their attention is constantly drawn away by external circumstances. Few people are internally motivated to change, and whenever motivation is externally initiated (e.g. through a partner's demands, or crisis caused by break-up), it is short-term and soon vanishes, usually as soon as the crisis is over and life returns to normal.

On the other hand, a rational decision to end a relationship does not necessarily solve the fundamental problem, i.e. our unconscious patterns. More often, we simply carry the same patterns into our next relationships. Sometimes, it can make more sense to use the chance to improve our communication skills, to recognize and work on our feelings, even if it is not likely that a particular relationship will last. However, do not linger in relationships in which you are hurt and abused.

If you are in a relationship with an abusive partner, or if you calmly feel that it is time to end a partnership – then probably it is. But, if you make a rational decision, while your feelings scream against it, maybe give yourself some time and work with your emotions, so that you can end the relationship peacefully. You will know when it will be an appropriate time to split up.

In my own relationships, I noticed that after I mastered some lessons, I started to feel attracted to relationships in which unresolved patterns were still present – but milder, with less drama and with more support from the partner. The realization that it is not necessary to solve every problem to have a happy and fulfilling relationship is very encouraging. Sometimes all it takes is a step or two, primarily in your relationship with yourself, to attract the relationship in which you can experience challenges in much easier and more pleasant ways.

Breaking up

Break ups (especially when initiated by the other person, or occurring because of external circumstances) provoke intense, deep and, in essence, childlike emotions. Sadness is a normal reaction to loss, but many people experience deeper crisis than would normally be considered healthy. At the surface, the pain arises out of a feeling of abandonment or rejection. Remember how you felt after a break up that you did not initiate and most likely, you will remember emotions you would not wish to revive. (If you ended a relationship, especially after a period of preparation, the feelings of abandonment are not as intense.)

Children experience everything around them intensely and tend to generalize with black and white conclusions. They are also less conscious of time, which can make even short-term abandonment in early childhood appear to last forever. If parents are also emotionally immature (many are to a certain extent), children will feel even more rejected or deserted. Similar feelings emerge in situations when we feel rejected as adults, but the deepest and most suppressed feelings penetrate the consciousness only when we end important intimate relationships.

Moreover, I believe that one of the causes of such patterns is the way that children are raised in our society. In many "primitive" societies, children are reared by the entire community. Such children receive love, security and support from many people and do not feel so dependent on one or two people. In our society, children are almost wholly dependent upon their parents. Sometimes grandparents or babysitters are around, but usually only occasionally. Separation from parents then provokes particularly strong feelings of fear and abandonment, which in adulthood can lead to stronger bonding and feeling of dependency in intimate relationships.

In their moments of crisis, people usually decide to do whatever they can to resolve it, but once the emotions subside and return to the subconscious, it is easy to forget their intensity and consequences. Instead, you may delude yourself that it was not so terrible or that it is now behind you. However, until you truly resolve your subconscious issues, you will continue to create or be attracted to situations that will bring them out.

"Our greatest problems contain our greatest blessings" (Martyn Carruthers) - and once we resolve the emotional dependency that comes from feelings of rejection, we can create balance and happiness, joy and love that is not so dependent on external circumstances.

Points to ponder:

What do you long for in a relationship, but repeatedly don't get?

Consider your past intimate relationships. Did they have a similar general atmosphere, communication style and unfulfilled needs? Perhaps they had similar positive aspects too? Did those relationships have similar qualities to your early relationship with your parents?

Are you trying to "save" your partner in some way? Do you try to be his or her therapist? (What would he/she say about this?) Do you try to deserve love in such ways?

Check your own behavior: how do you express your needs? How do you communicate when you are unsatisfied or angry? Do you show how you feel in indirect ways? Are there any similarities with the way your parents used to communicate, or have you developed your behavior through the experience you had with past partners?

Did you stay in unsatisfying relationships because of the potential you saw in your partners, or because of the idea of unconditional love - or something else?

Did you end relationships with anger and resentment? Or with cold aloofness? Or what? How do you feel about your ex partners? What is still unresolved? Do you have similar problems in your current partnership, if you are in one?

Practice:

Pay attention to your thoughts and behaviors when you feel irritated or frustrated. Consider how to change them. Can you directly, earnestly and calmly express your feelings, without blaming the other person? Do you fear how your partner might react to it? What does this remind you of?

If you have experienced major separation, which you feel is still not fully resolved, use the "Exploring Emotions" process in the appendix. You can do this with other unpleasant feelings and patterns too.

Partnership and Self-Esteem

Sometimes people ask me about the qualities they should seek in potential partners. This question deserves to be answered in detail, so here I offer a LONG answer.

I put self-esteem in the first place, as self-esteem influences all other areas of our lives. The problem is, it is not easy to find a person with healthy self-esteem. Much behavior that is commonly confused with expressions of self-love and confidence – e.g., insisting in being right, objecting to anything you do not like or arrogance - are compensating for a lack of true self-love. Very often, our subconscious self-image is toxic and our conscious self-perception is more or less neutral. In my opinion, very few people have an idea how different their lives would be if they felt true self-love.

Many people feel flattered and important if they sense that their partners need them or depend on them and would suffer if they separated. (Doesn't this sound like what is usually called romantic love?). However, those are indications that we are loved in infantile, not adult ways. Our partners may not see us as real, unique human beings, but as substitutes for important people from their pasts. In these cases, their love doesn't truly belong to us.

In such relationships, we lose our freedom to be who we truly are. Our partners are bonded to us, dependent on us playing our assigned roles. They expect us to replace someone else. Any deviation from that "someone else" creates fear; disrupts the relationship and leads to accusations and conflicts.

For emotionally healthy people, intimacy with emotionally mature partners who do not depend on their love, is a true compliment – it means their partners see and love **them**, not some fantasy figure. Yet, many people feel insecure in such relationships, because of popular beliefs that love requires codependency, fixations and perhaps obsessions.

If you notice that you melt with tenderness, or feel increased security, even superiority when you notice signs of low self-esteem, dependency, bonding, self-criticism, pessimism etc. in your partner – know that, to the same level, your partner is incapable of mature love and respect for you. This will probably cause problems in other areas of your relationship. People will treat you in similar ways to how they treat themselves - how they criticize themselves, ignore their own needs, consider their emotions to be unimportant, etc. On the other hand, the more people are prone to criticism, aggression, arrogance and inconsiderate behavior, the more they will treat their own deeper, gentler feelings in similar ways.

If you show pity and play the role of savior, you do not help your partner. This does not mean you should leave, or that it is OK to be cold and critical in those moments. Adult love means tactful and respectful compassion, confronting the people you love with reality and supporting their endeavors to become happy, independent adults.

The second place on my list of desirable qualities is commitment to continuous self improvement. The reason why this is not in first place is that a low self-esteem hinders change and independent thinking. It makes people dogmatic, compliant to authorities and more focused on formalities than on the essence of personal development. People who, even if unconsciously, do not value themselves, will likely value other people's opinions above their own, and perhaps sabotage changes that might increase their happiness, including the quality of their partnerships. That is why I find self-esteem to be more important for a successful relationship.

Self-esteem is a basis for optimism, a healthy sense of humor, communication skills and other qualities that make a good partner. Yet, even if we meet people who possess all those qualities – often we may not consider them as potential partners! We might appreciate those people, but we might not feel romantic attraction (unless perhaps if that person is unavailable for a relationship). Romantic love often binds us to people who trigger our unresolved patterns and problems. Many people who repeat unhealthy relationships find dramatic and immature behavior attractive because they associate it with love. Healthy people might bore them. Even if you are attracted to more mature people, you might do the same (although it might be harder to recognize if the patterns are subtle).

Can you easily and comfortably feel deep love for yourself? Do you trust that other people can truly, deeply and permanently love you? Do you have experience with people whom you loved, but who could not accept or trust your love? If we do not love ourselves, we cannot fully believe in other people's love.

When someone loves us, we do not "receive" their love directly; our awareness of that person's love amplifies and encourages our own healthy self-love. Only to the extent to which we love and appreciate ourselves, will we be able to feel the fullness and depth of love that connects other people to us.

In any case, we will feel attracted to people whose emotional maturity (almost a synonym for self-esteem) is in line with our own. This can help you understand how important it is to work on your emotional health first, rather than hoping that someone else would solve your problems.

"To find the person you want, first become that person".

Points to ponder:

Would you feel secure in a relationship with a partner who is happy and self-confident even when you are not?

How would you feel if your partner behaves in insecure, needy or even immature ways?

Do you feel that your partner appreciates and loves him or herself?

Practice:

Try to feel love for yourself. Is this easy and natural, or do you feel resistance?

Try to fully feel and accept your partner's love, or perhaps love from a friend or other people. Do you feel that you deserve it? Do you believe in the stability of their love, even when your behavior is not perfect?

Mature Responsibility

I often recommend Harville Hendrix as an author whose observations and descriptions of internal patterns and partnership issues, as well as family systems, are deep, detailed and to the point. Because of that, it is also important for me to emphasize some aspects in which I disagree with his theories.

Looking for a substitute parent

Although I deeply appreciate Hendrix's skills in recognizing causes of problems, I do not fully agree with the solutions he proposes. His approach is that it is desirable, if not necessary, that partners take responsibility for fulfilling each other's needs and healing each other's emotions. This is normally the responsibility of parents, so in this way partners end up switching between roles of parents, partners and children. This leads to emotional codependency, since we lean on someone else rather than on ourselves. Besides, we can put a huge burden on our partners that might feel like emotional blackmail, depending what we demand and how we communicate.

Unless both partners are very mature and well aware of their needs and demands, people using Hendrix's method can easily violate each other's boundaries and neglect each other's personalities. For example, a woman might ask a man to give up his hobbies and time alone for the sake of healing her childish needs, or a man could ask from a woman, in the name of love, to cook and clean most of the time.

An example from my practice is a couple who could not agree how to follow Hendrix's recommendations. The man wanted the woman to play sexual roles she found humiliating, and he would complain that he felt rejected and hurt if she did not. Partners who refuse such requests may be accused of not following the method and not wanting a better partnership.

In the short term, this kind of role playing can be enjoyable: we abandon ourselves to someone else, hoping that our needs will be fulfilled in ways we long for – with love, without pain and without a need to take responsibility for our own feelings. In the long run, however, this approach can diminish intimacy and passion between two adults and stimulate transferences, that is, seeing the partner as a parent rather than a unique human being.

In his book "Getting The Love You Want", Hendrix notices that many people, after initial excitement and renewal of warm feelings for their partners encouraged by this approach, become disillusioned and the old conflicts come back. At first, they see each other as "the one who has everything they need, an ideal partner that will miraculously make them whole". When the real person does not match this fantasy, they may experience disappointment and resentment. Hendrix's solution to this problem is that both partners should work on developing the qualities the other person wishes them to have, which can awaken their hidden or undeveloped potential. In theory, this sounds like a good way to use partnership for personal development – but is still not enough to heal the underlying issues, and involves a danger of forcing the partners to be who they do not want to be.

I think that both partners should use their relationship to recognize their own patterns, without requiring that their partners heal them. I prefer to work with causes rather than with consequences, where the latter logically takes more time, is harder and often unsuccessful. Healing can happen in cooperation with other people – but not through them. The main responsibility is our own.

Hendrix claims that we cannot heal ourselves without long-term support from another person, since our unconscious minds need external experience with another human being as a replacement for parents, to be able to change. I agree that real world experiences are important to complete the healing process, but we have to take the responsibility for the most important part of the work.

One of the biggest disadvantages of Hendrix's approach is that it does not provide a solution for people whose partners do not want to change (which is common!), or for people who choose relationships in which such intimacy and mutual commitment is not possible: for example people who bond to addicts, abusers, or to unavailable or immature individuals.

This is a high percentage of people who, if it was true that only a relationship with a supportive partner could heal them, would be left without hope. Even if they left their current partners, hoping that they could find another person to heal with, they would continue to be attracted to people with similar patterns. Some of these people are single

114

for years – should they waste more years until they find someone who could give them a chance to heal? Similarly, Hendrix's approach would imply that limiting beliefs in other areas of life cannot be resolved without changing the outer circumstances first – which is unrealistic.

Unhealthy responsibility

Most of us are strongly conditioned by our childhoods and by unpleasant, sometimes almost unbearable emotions coming from our "inner children". Some people use their childhoods as an excuse for not taking responsibility, or for shifting it onto someone else, perhaps retreating into self-pity. As children, we had little choice – while as adults we are responsible for how we deal with emotions and circumstances. Adults who assume other adults' responsibilities, usually create damaging consequences for both themselves and the others in the long run. Too much help often encourages people to become dependent, thus reducing their ability to develop their own resources. They might learn to act like victims to attract sympathy and support, and avoid dealing with their issues.

People in romantic relationships often take responsibility for their partners' feelings. This may be expected and perceived as evidence of love. Yet healthy people will see such added responsibilities as intrusive and a burden. Have you ever taken responsibility for an adult's feelings and needs? If you have ever been in this position, you know how it feels.

For example, it is unhealthy for children to feel responsible for their parents' emotions. Parents should be more mature and much more capable to take care of their own needs. Unfortunately, many parents think it is natural to at least partly burden even small children with their feelings, by playing victims. This makes children feel guilty and conflicted between healthy reactions and unhealthy imposed responsibilities, creating patterns that continue into adulthood. As adults, they might be able to make healthier decisions – but rarely without feeling guilty.

Suzanne, although she was a planned child, was often told by her mother: "You enslaved me, you took all my time and energy". As an adult, she felt that it was her duty to care for her mother, please her and give her much more than necessary. She felt that her life purpose was to submit herself to others. But she was also aware of her anger about that idea, and she expressed it with the words, "People have children so that they have someone to take care of them later!" Due to her deep guilt, it was difficult for her to let go of her patterns, but with time she progressed and she learned to feel confident enough to set boundaries and to calmly, without guilt or need for revenge, explain to her mother what was and what was not acceptable to her.

Concern or guilt about how other people feel (if it is not a result of our immature behavior), or trying to make people feel better, means that we cease seeing those people as strong adults. Instead, we see them as children who cannot handle their lives and emotions without help. Since our society, on average, is quite immature, many people find such behavior to be normal or even desirable, as it provides temporary relief. However, if you have experienced how it feels when someone imposes help on you that you do not want – probably you felt underestimated by their pity or lack of trust in your ability, no matter how nice were their intentions.

By assuming responsibility for other people, we also take away their power – sending a message that we do not consider them to be strong, mature and capable. If we have such habits, we will probably compensate for them in other situations, and expect others to assume some of our responsibilities. Maybe the most effective assistance we can offer is to encourage adults in our lives to accept their responsibilities and use their power. We can do a big favor to ourselves if we stop accusing people or circumstances for our feelings, and if we recognize that any pleasure we obtain by pitying able adults is unhealthy.

Healthy support

Healthy compassion enables us to better understand people, especially those who struggle with their problems, just as we struggle with ours. It motivates us to support their efforts to heal themselves. While I believe that we are all responsible for our own feelings and behavior, some people use this as an excuse to avoid their responsibility for thoughtful behavior in relationships. They may believe, "If people are responsible for their own feelings, I can do whatever I like. If they don't feel good about what I do, that's their problem". They forget that they are still responsible for their own behavior. This happens not only in individual relationships, but also on local and global scales.

Such people may fear intimacy and responsibility. They will avoid considering other people's needs and boundaries. Such behavior may originate in: a) being spoiled and pampered as children, or b) rebelling against suppressed guilt and excessive responsibility for other people.

These people may have experienced intense manipulation. Guilt and imposed responsibility for the feelings of others in their childhood can lead to resisting any responsibility once they become independent. Such guilt can be so unpleasant that people avoid every possibility of becoming conscious of it.

Refusal to assume other people's responsibilities should not be confused with refusing to show love and support or to fulfill healthy partnership needs. To keep this sensitive balance, you need (again...) to carefully observe your own emotions and to discriminate healthy and appropriate desires from wanting to avoid responsibility.

Many people hope that if they improve enough, their partners will spontaneously improve too. This is rarely realistic. If one person changes quickly, and the other slowly, or not at all, the relationship can slide towards crisis. This is a risk of personal development - a risk that may include instability in relationships or finances. Awareness of this risk could negatively impact on our own progress.

Experiences of quality relationships are essential to maturity and happiness. Similarly, in any form of personal development, changing behavior, confronting problems in different ways, is also essential to complete integration. However, we need to invest our own awareness and efforts into our development, instead of waiting for others to do it for us.

Hoping that your partner will heal you can create dependency. People should first focus on resolving their own issues. Later, if their partners agree, they can help each other finish that process. Partners can consciously change their behavior to support each other in ways that also support their own integrity and identities.

Practice:
Notice the moments when you pity other people, or try to help or instruct them. Check how you see those people in those moments: as weak and immature, or as healthy and able? How do you imagine that

117

those people would prefer to be seen? If appropriate, talk to them about it.

Write down what you wish and need from a partnership and discuss the list with your partner. Focus on identifying needs that would be healthy to resolve on your own, and wishes that can improve the relationship.

Jealousy and Possessiveness

Jealousy is usually the most childish emotion of all. Fear, anger, sadness, shame and similar emotions can be caused by outer experiences and may be appropriate. (Most emotions reflect a mixture of both realistic and exaggerated childish perceptions). Jealousy, however, is most often based on infantile, black and white idea of not being good enough. It makes us feel that our sense of worth and self-esteem depend of other people's choices.

Although possessiveness towards intimate partners has some roots in biology and evolution, the essence of jealousy is a fear that we are not worthy of love, that something is wrong with us, that we will be rejected in favor of someone else. We might also feel that love and attention is in limited supply: if one person is receiving some, another has to lose. As a defense from our low self-image, we may start to build anger towards people who may "steal" love from us, and perhaps even towards the person whose love we want.

If your partner loved another person, how would you respond? Perhaps you would judge and blame the third person ruthlessly, especially if he/she dared to accept your partner's love. (When I write "love", I do not mean irresponsible sex or selfish behavior.) Often we hear pathetic claims such as: "he stole what was most important to me" or "she ruined my life".

Such victim talk is more appropriate for the immature lyrics of popular music than for adult communication. In many societies adultery was (or still is) punished by a slow and painful death. Imagine the power of childish fears and unworthiness, that they could makes whole societies ready to kill human beings for loving somebody other than a legal spouse!

Even in more sophisticated societies, individuals can still react to such experiences in dramatic ways. Some people are so afraid of losing a partner's love that they would do almost anything to prevent it. Such obsessions can motivate possessive behavior: perhaps controlling and isolating partners from other people; usually people of opposite sex, but occasionally from all social contacts. They might be jealous not only of people who might be potential lovers, but also the partners' families, same sex friends, even their own children.

Some of these people want to get rid of their jealousy, but do not know how: no rational decision is enough. Others believe that their jealousy is normal and justified.

Jealousy can trigger extremely abusive or even paranoid behavior, such as sabotaging a partner's hobbies and interests, suspicious questioning, accusations, criticism, humiliating a partner in public, blackmail and physical violence. A healthy intimate partnership is a relationship between two people who are aware that they chose each other because of their qualities and shared values. Such partners are also aware that those qualities can change with time and that their partners can feel friendly towards other people. Instead, exaggerated jealousy may turn relationships into imprisonment, ownership or abuse.

Those people who, as children, were encouraged to build self-esteem, a deep background feeling that they deserve love, are aware that their value does not depend on other people's choices. Thus, they can feel good about themselves when people they love are friendly to others. They will not feel an overwhelming need to be overly "special" to their beloved. It is what children want from parents. They will be aware that we can like different people in different ways. On the other hand, people with less self-esteem are more likely to feel emptiness, shame and fear of loss in such situations. They might use jealousy and possessiveness to avoid such emotions.

I am not trying to promote open marriages or irresponsible sex - even if free love (is that an oxymoron?) might be a rational ideal, we are more emotional than rational by nature. I believe it is wise to recognize and dissolve any attraction based on childish emotions, transferences or sexuality. Yet we cannot control all of our emotions, except by suppression or medication, which can have toxic consequences.

I have met people - mostly women - whose partners used logical ideals of free love, to talk them into allowing them to sleep with other people. Not only did such women suppress and deny their own feelings, but they lost the feeling of stability and confidence in their partners, which damages intimacy. That became a background for resentment and mistrust.

We are shaped by our childhoods, our experiences and our emotional needs. It is not wise to deny this. Most ideas can be abused and pushed into unhealthy extremes. I believe a healthy attitude is allowing your partner to choose – and then deciding whether or not you will stay with that person.

From a biological point of view, a woman needs a stable partner while raising children. Men often express a higher urge for promiscuity, yet raising children to healthy independence requires 15 or more demanding years. Perhaps we are biologically selected for long-term relationships, even if biological diversity allows for discrepancies. If promiscuity was normal, as with most species, romantic love might be measured in minutes. However, most men and most women prefer long-term monogamous relationships – at least after a certain period of experimenting is over.

Some biological instincts were useful in the past, but now are destructive and need to be controlled or sublimated (power and territory struggles, for example). Monogamous partnerships, however, continue to fulfill a purpose of raising healthy children. Besides, complex creatures as we are, it is difficult enough to achieve true intimacy with one person; spreading intimate attention to several people is practically impossible without greatly reducing the quality of relationships.

Biologically motivated jealousy is usually far milder than childish obsessions. It leaves space for healthy decisions and healthy self-image. Most of the time, jealousy is proportional and directly related to a negative self-image. This does not have to be obvious and conscious; most people suppress their unpleasant beliefs about themselves, perhaps hiding them under masks of arrogance and power.

Confident behavior is not the same as self-esteem. Many people learn how to be externally confident without the background of a healthy self-image. A better indication of self-esteem is how much we appreciate other people, not only ourselves. Negative opinions about ourselves usually prevent us from respecting others; we may avoid our feelings of inferiority by trying to belittle other people in our thoughts or in our behaviors.

If we truly like and appreciate ourselves, if we feel that we deserve love, we will expect it to be natural and easy to find people to love and who will love us. We will not experience the end of an important relationship as the "end of the world", even as we go through a period of sadness and emotional separation. We can also feel more respect, understanding and compassion for our partners and give them a similar freedom to what we want for ourselves.

Jealousy and family background

A common trigger of jealousy is the birth of a new child in a family. Children who feel lack of love and attention, will find it easiest to blame the new child. For the first child, the birth of the second can be a shock; not only most of parents' and other people's attention is suddenly transferred to the new child, but the older child may be given new responsibilities and expectations which might further increase insecurity ("you must help your little sister...").

The younger child, on the other hand, might perceive the older child as the one who is given more respect, trust and privileges, and thus develop a sense of inferiority and envy. As usual, grass is always greener on the other side of the fence!

Jealousy appears to be particularly strong amongst children of the same sex. Perhaps this is because children of different sex need different kinds of attention, so they do not feel so threatened by the type of attention given to the sibling. Another reason might be that, in the period of developing sexual roles (characterized by increased attachment to the opposite sex parent), boys and girls bond to different parents, so feelings of competition are not so strong.

Jealousy amongst children seems to be stronger if the age difference is small. Sometimes parents truly favor one child over the other. In the past, this was usually sons over daughters, which is still common in some cultures, but nowadays an increasing number of parents prefer daughters over sons. Ideally, of course, parents love all their children equally, but since there are no perfect people, the exceptions rule.

Every family is different and no common rule applies to everybody. A lot depends on age difference between children, as well as the parents' ability to express healthy love and warmth. The older a child is and the more love parents show, the less likely that their children will develop feelings of inadequacy and consequential jealousy.

Some children feel jealous of a parent, often the same sex parent. This kind of jealousy is normally less intense and children may be ashamed of it and avoid expressing it. Children can feel much more confused and guilty about such jealousy, than when it is about a sibling. A child is aware that in some way he is an "intruder" in an adult relationship, so he will usually hide such feelings, even from himself.

122

Such feelings usually appear from the age of three to six, when children develop awareness of their own sexuality. Opposite sex parents become more and more attractive, because through such attraction children explore their own sexuality. They may perceive a same sex parent as competition. Then a child might fantasize this parent somehow disappearing, or allowing the child to take the parent's place. Children sometimes say things like "When I grow up, I'll marry Dad!" or "Mom, you're my wife!" If the parents react calmly and lovingly, but while discouraging such ideas, the child can go through this phase without creating lasting patterns of inadequacy and jealousy.

If a family is chaotic and unhealthy, a child might develop a toxic bond to a parent. Such children might obsessively search for love and attention. They might hope that they will be able to "save" their parents and make them happy. If a child perceives a parent as a victim, that child might hope to prove to the parent that she can make him happier than the other parent can. If the parent encourages this through a pattern called "covert emotional incest" (which I have written about earlier in this book), jealousy might become a lasting and truly toxic issue.

Later, as adults, such children might feel strongly attracted to "love triangles" and situations of competing with others for the love of their partners. They might want to get rid of jealousy, but as long as they hold subconscious images of needy parents, jealousy will persist.

If you want to overcome jealousy, a key is to develop a sense of worthiness and a feeling that being loved is normal. Of course, that will create positive consequences in many other areas of your life.

Points to ponder:

Do you think that jealousy is appropriate in certain situations? If yes, which ones? Could there be healthier and more constructive responses?

Consider what might be healthy and constructive ways to express your jealousy (besides running in circles, screaming and shouting).

What do you think is appropriate to expect in a partnership? Do you believe you and your partner "own" each other? What might be a realistic limit of controlling one's emotions? Where does friendliness end and intimacy begin?

Practice:

Remember situations when you felt jealousy. Which emotions were included in that state? Perhaps fear, anger, feeling of inadequacy... What age were your emotions appropriate for?

What were you most afraid of? Abandonment, betrayal, somebody else being "better" than you, losing financial security...? If that happened, how would you feel? Perhaps humiliated, not good enough, like your world is falling apart or like life does not make sense anymore? What might be the background of such experiences? Do they remind you of anything from your past?

If you are jealous, consider your partner's perspective. Perhaps from his/her point of view, you have nothing to worry about? Or perhaps he/she is not committed to your partnership and does not take responsibility for inconsiderate behavior? If you felt worthy, resourceful and at peace with yourself, how would you respond?

Consider if your partner's behavior might be a symptom of ignored problems in your relationship. It might be taking each other for granted, criticism, unresolved conflicts, low quality communication or perhaps something else?

Keeping Passion Alive

After several years of relationship, most couples start taking each other for granted and stop doing little things, which helped them, win their partner's appreciation and approval in the earlier stages of the relationship. How can we prevent this loss of passion in a relationship or marriage?

In the first place, as much as possible, take care to think about your partner in the way you did in the beginning. Notice qualities you like and be compassionate to idiosyncrasies that do not burden or threaten you. If you find some parts of your partner's behavior upsetting, consider if they may be irrelevant details that remind you of earlier unpleasant experiences, or are they signs of irresponsibility or neglect.

Besides your respect and delight for a partner's qualities, passion stems from sexual attraction - which often diminishes after the birth of children. Many women focus on children, and even if they try to be attentive to their partners too, they will often be too tired and unfocused. In the first few years of a child's life, you might need to accept the fact that you have less time for each other. But as children grow up, it is important that parents enliven their relationships. Keeping sexual attraction alive often means encouraging men to feel masculine, and women to feel feminine, while avoiding rigid and burdensome prejudice.

Most men feel particularly masculine when they can actively support their partners' happiness, receive their gratitude and feel wanted and needed. Most women feel feminine when they feel understood, supported and safe to relax.

Through millions of years of evolution, women were mostly focused on vulnerable children and their dangerous environments, while men physically protected and helped them. Many women in modern society feel that too much responsibility is placed on them: jobs, children, housework ... if they cannot relax and do not feel supported, they stop feeling feminine. This creates dissatisfaction and resentment, which few women can explain.

Such resentment may motivate *nagging*. A woman who feels that she cannot relax and that the man's support is lacking, might be unable to explain it to him, and might express her tension and frustration by criticizing details of her partner's behavior. On the other side, men are encouraged (by marketing, television and role models) to be more self-indulgent than before. This reduces the traditional male support to women, and men can lose their sense of masculinity. They may become passive, or confused by female demands.

New solutions for old needs

I am certainly not trying to say that people should return to traditional life-styles. This would reduce possibilities for women to explore the other aspects of their personalities besides motherhood. People are not just biological reproduction machines, but much more complex. Focusing on one aspect of existence while neglecting the others, is unhealthy. In the same way, a rigid focus on biological roles only is unhealthy. An advantage of modern society is the physical and material independence of women, which gives them more choice and opportunity than ever before. Giving that independence up, avoiding responsibility, is not only unhealthy for a woman, but reflects on her partner and children.

Instead, we need to create new models of behavior, through which men can feel that they have important roles in their families and can help their partners relax. (I sometimes hear men complain that their sole function in their family is to pay the bills.) As the modern way of life is more complex than ever before, it makes no sense for me to offer detailed advice here. It is better if we ask our partners what helps them feel more masculine/feminine, and if we explain which behaviors are more likely to encourage complementary feelings in us and trigger romance. It is important to avoid rigid demands and instead make time for playful exploration.

Again - Do not get me wrong: I do not advocate rigid gender roles, which created so much suffering and humiliation in the past. Even with all the unpleasant aspects of modern society, we have much more physical security, freedom of choice and opportunity to explore more sophisticated aspects of our lives and personalities. Still, the instincts we developed through evolution are still with us, and although (luckily!) they do not need to be in control of our behavior, we can use them wisely to increase romance and passion.

Maintain a playful attitude instead of making rigid demands. Flexibility is a foundation of good relationships - at least when it comes to details. Important life values are another matter. I meet too many people

126

who fight bitterly about details (e.g. how to cut butter, or the famous toilet seat position). Sometimes you need to consider whether those details are important enough to endanger the quality of your partnership.

Does your partner, against all your reasons and pleas, avoid putting food back into the fridge or dirty dishes into the sink? Such behaviors do not mean that your partner is a bad or irresponsible person. Many relationships fail because partners attribute bad intentions to each other, on the basis of petty habits. (E.g. "He only does that to annoy me!") Can we show understanding and compassion to our partners, giving space when they are in a bad mood, irritable, and generally not at their best? Then we can continue building mutual trust, respect and motivation to put effort in our relationships ... with emotionally healthy people at least.

Differences in how we express love can often create misunderstandings. Some people express their feelings through words and conversation, while others need physical touch or shared activities. Some people regard gifts to be an important expression of love, while to other people, gifts are a nuisance. If you do not notice how your partner expresses love to you, because you learned that love is expressed in different ways ... discuss this with your partner. Appreciate good intentions, even if the behavior is not exactly what you would prefer. In this way, you can minimize unnecessary conflicts.

When is enough - enough?

People who do not trust their own instincts may allow themselves to be manipulated into tolerating being neglected, humiliated and controlled. Some women believe that being independent and giving space to their partners means accepting their lack of responsibility and consideration. Some people are manipulated into believing that they are selfish, uncaring and irresponsible if they do not fulfill their partner's every wish. Some couples just do not recognize that they are not compatible, and waste time criticizing, blaming or trying to change each other.

If you are a man and want to make your partner happy, but are unsure how to distinguish between acting either as a husband or a father, consider the questions that follow. These questions can also help women who are not sure whether they demand too much, or are their partners just acting like fragile plants in a sensitive process of bonding to a couch:

- Is your partner generally independent and responsible, or does she expect other people (primarily you) to take responsibility for her needs, feelings and desires?

- Is she flexible and tolerant if everything does not go her way, or does she criticize and belittle you for not reading her mind?

- Does she express her expectations and complaints in calm and relaxed ways, or by playing victim, manipulating or becoming aggressive?

- Do you feel that you have found a balance in sharing work and responsibilities, or do you feel that almost everything is on you (or on your partner)?

- Is it pleasurable and fulfilling for you to do things for her, or is it a burden and obligation? Does she express pleasure and appreciation when you help her, or do you feel that you cannot do anything well enough?

If you prefer rational analysis instead of listening to your intuition, it might be difficult for you to find answers. Listen to your feelings - not only to the superficial and often defensive ones, but to your deeper feelings, which are usually calmer and more comprehensive. Recognize that partnership is not symbiosis, that you are still two adults who are responsible for your own lives and needs. Partnership means cooperation - while preserving a sense of personal space and boundaries. Only then can we feel a healthy passion.

Quality Communication

Few people are aware of their body language. The more we pay attention to **how** people communicate, the more we notice how much human interaction we usually miss. People send many messages by nonverbal signals, for example by the tonality of their voices as opposed to their choice of words. You can greatly improve your relationships by noticing and interpreting these messages - especially those from people who do not express themselves clearly and candidly.

Do you ever "get lost" in simple conversations and find yourself arguing with someone about something that, in essence, you both agree with?

Many misunderstandings occur when people ignore non-verbal signals. They may end up asking or answering wrong questions at the wrong time. Probably everyone has experienced the confusion of feeling confident that a talk ended well, but hearing later that the other person was not pleased.

Sometimes important things can be explained and disputes avoided if we recognize small problems, understand what the other person is communicating, or find the right words to explain our position. As with many other important aspects of life, few people take time to deal with such issues.

For example, I once made a remark about a specific behavior pattern and gave my opinion about its cause. At that moment, I noticed that the friend I was talking to stiffened and frowned, but the moment passed quickly and the conversation continued normally. I did not think about it until a few weeks later when I found out that my friend had thought that my remark was about her. Left unresolved, this could have spoiled our relationship.

Another friend and I agreed to resolve all kinds of misunderstandings as quickly and openly as possible. She sometimes asks me what do I think about things she said, concerned that I might misunderstand her. It usually turns out that everything is fine, but this kind of checking and resolving small doubts creates trust and closeness, even if explanations are unnecessary. This reminds us both that we value our relationship and care for each other.

Many people, when they are not sure what to say, attempt to answer too quickly. They respond with half-considered thoughts, clichés, empty witticisms, provocations, or simply withdraw to avoid conflict. Instead of all that, you can listen to your body's emotional signals. If you pay attention to your "gut feelings" and translate them into words, you can often recognize important problems and find appropriate reactions. This skill of inner awareness requires practice, given that in the midst of communication our focus is mostly external, which makes it more difficult to recognize subtle psychosomatic signals.

Self-control or spontaneity

People often say that they do not want to control themselves, rather that they want to relax and be spontaneous. This conflict between spontaneity and quality communication is common if we invest time and energy in learning new skills.

My experience shows, and this is easy to recognize amongst most people, that spontaneous and automatic reactions are more often than not acquired defense mechanisms or expressions learned from our surroundings. Our answers and behavior before we think things over, almost before we even notice, may not be honest expressions of what and who we are. Therefore, it is important to learn not to react automatically. We need to give ourselves time to feel what we truly want to communicate ... providing that we have learned to be truthful to ourselves. (Perhaps quality spontaneity is not so spontaneous.)

Many people, however, are afraid to take time before responding to problematic communications. Many children learn that other people may utilize such time to "outplay" and "defeat" them in communication. The reality is often different: in many situations, the other person feels no need to do this. By giving ourselves time we send messages on several levels. First, that we care about the outcome of our communication and that we are thinking carefully about what was said and what we would say; secondly, that we are aware, present and acting with honesty (which means that we maintain an attitude of self-esteem). Moreover, in many situations when people express their views hastily and inappropriately, the time that we take to consider an answer often allows those people to evaluate their own behavior.

Nonverbal communication

Nonverbal communication can give us important signals: not only of consciously repressed feelings and thoughts, but also of unconscious dynamics. However, we need to avoid the trap of perceiving ourselves as the ultimate interpreters of nonverbal signals and convincing ourselves that specific signals represent exactly what we think they do. Ambitious observers of nonverbal communication can be annoying when they try to convince you that you think what they think that you think. Avoid becoming one of them.

A good approach is to compare each gesture and expression with other elements of communication, instead of interpreting them separately. Moreover, our feelings are not influenced only by the current situation, but also by our coincidental thoughts, associations and memories. Add discomfort to this, if we are aware of being observed (such discomfort may increase if people give hasty interpretations of our signals!) Similarly, when on a lie detector, innocent people can show higher levels of stress than the guilty, if they are afraid that they might be misunderstood and falsely accused. As in many other aspects of life, we will often get better insights about other people's nonverbal communication if we let the interpretation come through our feelings and intuitive impressions, rather than through conscious and rational analysis. Our subconscious minds include decades of intense learning experiences, as well as inherited instincts; our rational minds do not.

If we consciously try to control our nonverbal communications, perhaps to project feelings we don't truly feel, we will fail, unless we are really good actors. Unconscious minds cannot lie – lies are conscious decisions – so even if we manage to control some parts of our bodies, other parts will give us away. What we should work on – for the sake of our integrity more than external results – is to truly develop within us the feelings we wish to show non-verbally.

Every communication with other people, everything we say and how we say it, influences our relationships and future conversations, i.e., how much will someone trust us next time and feel relaxed and open with us. It is easy to escape into "spiritual realms" - yet we expose our spiritual progress in our everyday communication.

Whom are we actually talking to?

In every communication, try to remember that you perceive only one part, or one sub-personality of the other person! Many times, what we say under the influence of temporary emotions, is not what we normally think and believe. You can create certain impressions about people solely based on a few things they say, while afterwards their behavior might reveal rather different traits. A good example could be the difference in our behavior and communication when we are in love with someone, as compared with when we slowly return to routine and "normal" parts of our personalities take over.

Just as in our relationship with ourselves, communication with others requires time and consistency at training deep awareness and sensitivity to details. It is even more difficult to learn to express our feelings in sincere yet compassionate ways. But once we learn how to do it, our relationships – the most important basis for a quality life – have a chance to blossom.

Points to ponder:

Do you sometimes notice unusual non-verbal reactions of people you talk to? What do you do next?

How do you feel in emotionally intense situations, when you cannot find a quick answer? What do you do then? What do you think might happen if you took time to think before answering?

Do you enjoy interpreting nonverbal communications? How do you feel when you notice that someone is observing your nonverbal communication?

Practice:

Practice being fully present and focused on your feelings, while at the same time observing nonverbal communications of people you talk to. Try to always take some time to find the right words. What difficulties do you have when you try this?

Observe your automatic reactions in emotionally intense situations, and what you say without forethought. Are those words the most appropriate and healthy for those situations? Whom do those reactions remind you of? Whom did you learn them from?

When you observe nonverbal communications, consider if those nonverbal signals could have other meanings, beside whatever comes first to your mind.

Remember a comment that hurt you. Consider how much of the person was represented in that statement? Maybe just a small part, or perhaps a considerably big one?

Communication Skills, Power and Manipulation

Probably you have noticed, from time to time, books and workshops advertised with pompous promises such as: 'take control in all communications', 'get people to do things you want them to do', ' develop magnetic attraction' and so on.

Everything we do or say influences other people, even without our conscious awareness or wanting to. Hence the authors of such books might say: since we already do this, why not gain some benefit? I read an article about a man who runs workshops for men on seducing women. Amongst other things, he wrote that men can use his methods to encourage women to be more self-confident, or that by using specific words a man can suggest that a woman is spontaneous, has an adventurous spirit, is relaxed, etc. and that there is nothing negative about this. However, the purpose of those "encouragements" is to provoke insecure women to prove themselves "spontaneous and adventurous" by accepting his other suggestions.

Communication skills are incredibly important in human relationships. With careless communication we can create any number of misunderstandings and problems. Often, though, there is a thin line between improving relationships, and influencing people to do things they do not want to do, especially if they are not aware of the manipulation.

For example, parents who use communication techniques with their children often do not use them in honest attempts to understand what their children want and feel, but to control their behavior. In the former example of seduction workshops, such methods are used to encourage sexual intimacy while hiding one's true intentions and without considering the possible consequences for the manipulated women.

Such techniques may also be used to make women more likely to "fall in love", before they have had a chance to get to know a man better and to judge how much they really like him. Furthermore, men in those workshops were encouraged to make women feel insecure and increase their desire to fulfill expectations.

Promoters of manipulative communication might claim that it can actually help people. (Some people seem to use their brains mostly as excuse-making machines.) If you succeed in making other people want to behave in the way you want, or to feel better about themselves – it is supposed to be good for them. This disrespectful attitude implies that we know better what is good for other people than they do. This egotistical viewpoint can have unpleasant consequences even in parent - child relationships, and especially in adult relationships.

Even if you believe that you are trying to prevent someone from making a mistake - people often need mistakes. How else can we learn, if not from experience?

Even if we think that we are doing good, we need to ask ourselves if we can really feel good and if we have a clear conscience, knowing that we have influenced other people without their knowledge? Is it possible to truly respect others, if we, through purposeful control, put them in positions of weaker, manipulated people?

In such relationships, honesty and intimacy are not likely to occur. On the other hand, is it even possible to influence other people with their full knowledge and agreement, if we often do not realize how we influence others?

Perhaps the more you try to hide from people that you want to influence them, the less you can respect those people. Communication skills are the most honest and respectful if we apply them without hiding our intentions. Personally, for my own integrity, I favor approaches that are not designed to awaken certain emotions or responses, but rather to help people to consciously and independently consider both their own and my viewpoints.

Need for power

The need for power is within all people. We desire to "shine", to be attractive to others, to feel powerful. All people enjoy such fantasies and it is easy to justify attempts to achieve them. A question that few people consider is, where does this need come from? What is missing that makes us seek such reassurances? Why do we only feel worthy enough when we feel special or better than others? Working on our self-esteem rather than on some external image may save us not only years but decades of effort.

Moreover, no external success can permanently change the way we feel about ourselves. Self-esteem must come from within, not without. Such a feeling is incomparably better than power over others. When you have healthy self-esteem, you will likely act in ways that will motivate others to value and love you deeper than you could achieve using any type of trickery.

As a rule, if you feel subtly manipulated in a conversation, even if you do not know in which way – you probably are. Practically any communication skill can be used dishonestly. The key is the **intention** and the **attitude** of the other person, even when their external behavior might be difficult to recognize as manipulative. Yet it is almost impossible to play that game without tiny non-verbal signals giving us away: minimal changes in the tone of voice, stiff smiles and facial expressions, tiny abrupt movements, use of clichés instead of spontaneous words – all of these may be signals that people do not notice consciously but unconsciously they will.

In such cases, usually there are intuitive feelings, such as, "Something feels strange about this, but I'm not sure what". The sooner we notice and interpret those feelings, the better. To do this efficiently and immediately, if possible, we need to train ourselves to notice and interpret our own feelings.

To avoid being manipulated, it is often a good idea to say that you need time to think (for example when somebody asks for a favor or if you are being persuaded to make a purchase). You can say that you will be back after you have given the suggestion some thought. Go outside, take a walk and contemplate your decision without external pressure.

It is so much easier to live with honesty, instead of having to rigidly control ourselves, to pretend emotions that we do not really feel, to constantly pay attention to whether we missed something or if somebody might see through our act. Do you really want to invest so much energy into manipulation? Could the desire to manipulate people indicate a deeper emotional problem?

If you are playing a short-term game, you probably do not care about the consequences on the other person. Another possibility is that you want to keep people around you continuously impressed (you want to be charismatic), so that you can feel important and powerful. In this case, disrespect for others, as well as disrespect for yourself, might be unconscious - a feeling of not being worthy or important enough, which you hide by attempting to control others.

People without healthy self-esteem are attracted to methods, books and workshops offering power and charisma. They hope to fill an inner void created by deep beliefs that they cannot attract love and appreciation without some form of pretense.

I mentioned seduction methods. Some seduction methods are common and even expected "mating rituals": flirting, gifts, emphasizing physical attributes, compliments... Sometimes, the seducer might be honestly interested, and sometimes selfishly, but since the behavior is the same, it can be difficult to distinguish one from the other. A "seduced" person might want to believe in the other's honesty and might enjoy the attention and good feelings. Such a person might hope that a "seducer" is using stereotypical behaviors because these are normal and familiar ways to be romantic.

Sometimes it is so, yet I believe that the more naturally and spontaneously people express their romantic feelings, the more likely that they are honest and open in other areas of their lives. Their healthy self-esteem allows them to be unguarded. For additional help in estimating the worthiness of potential partners, observe how they communicate with people they do not find important (cashiers, passers-by and other drivers in traffic). When the romance wears off, they may treat you in similar ways.

When you use specific communication skills, ask yourself if you are using them to hide your true intention and feelings, or to express yourself in the most appropriate way? Every time we use our communication skills to avoid being honest and open, we reject our own true selves and miss a chance to accept ourselves. Also, in the future, it will become more difficult to respect yourself, knowing how you have used people without caring about the consequences they would suffer.

I think that it is impossible to use manipulative approaches while simultaneously respecting people. If you respect other people, conscious manipulation is practically impossible, because the attempt to influence another person with your hidden agenda involves disrespect. To justify such attempts to ourselves, we have to devalue our understanding of the worth or abilities of other people. Since our approach to others reflects the way we perceive ourselves, by devaluing others we lower our own self-esteem too.

A price for manipulating people - even if you manage to achieve it - is that you can never relax and be yourself. You will be under constant pressure to maintain an illusion, not only in relationships with others, but also within yourself. You will be constantly on guard and worrying if people might finally see through you. What the authors of all those books on charisma and persuasion won't tell you, is that controlling others presumes much worse, painful control over the most honest and authentic parts of you. Perhaps there are a few better examples of the "boomerang - effect" than these methods of controlling others.

If you are tempted to try these kinds of games, ask yourself: do you want relaxed, spontaneous relationships with healthy people (who would not tolerate such games), people who see you and appreciate you as you are - or do you want to see people as puppets? Do you want to mold people to fit your fantasies? Then you will attract immature people to you - people who tolerate such games and pretense, people who might ignore you if you relax.

Whenever I met people who manipulate others, even if they had succeeded in getting some power and influence over others, I never felt that they were happy, truly liking and appreciating themselves. The price of being a successful manipulator is that other people might like or even admire your act, your false projection, but not your true self.

The more you manipulate others, the more you will manipulate yourself and the more difficult it will be to enjoy being who you really are. **The price you pay is your self-esteem**, because, no matter how much you deny or justify it, you know you cheat people. On the other hand, I occasionally meet people who radiate true charisma. Their attractiveness is based on healthy self-esteem - accepting who they are and enjoying their existence.

Points to ponder:

How do you feel when advertisements promise that you can control others through communication techniques, become more attractive to others, or get the results you want without other people knowing that you manipulated them?

In that case, how would your perception of other people change?

Check your feelings - would this really feel good?

How did it feel when someone manipulated or attempted to manipulate you? How did you recognize this? How do you think that the other person perceived you in that moment? What do you think of those people now?

Spirituality

Being Your Own Authority

One of the most valuable lessons in life, in my opinion, is learning to trust yourself and to listen to your inner voice, rather than anybody else's. If you uncritically accept other people's beliefs and opinions (we know how normal this is in childhood, and how much of their true selves children can lose), you renounce your own responsibility and power. Then not even your successes are your own. You can probably remember examples from your own life, when you trusted the ideas and opinions of specific other people, only to realize eventually, whether in an easier or more difficult way, that they didn't have all the answers and that their truth isn't necessarily yours. This is a very important lesson and I believe that everybody needs such an experience, often more than once.

Not even the authorities you most respect will always have the best answers. Nobody in the world can know it all, even if you see them as enlightened. Even if they could, there is always the question of whether there is such a thing as an absolute truth applicable to any situation. If such truths exist, then I believe them to be small in number. Maybe you have experienced a situation when you felt an inner urge to do something that was not quite attuned to your beliefs, only to realize after some time that that action created more benefit for both you and other people, than if you had stuck rigidly to your beliefs. Life is endlessly diverse; people, relationships and circumstances are unique and our inner voices can access a much wider source of information than our rational minds.

Pleasing authority

Most religions and spiritual approaches require obeying a great number of rules, sometimes very petty ones, striving to control every aspect of human life. This, perhaps purposefully, does not allow much space for listening to your inner voice. I believe that, while seeking security and trying to build self-esteem through following such rules, people unconsciously strive to please a spiritual authority (whether a living person or a spiritual ideal) in a similar way to how they tried to please their parents during childhood. If this requires suppressing our healthy urges and feelings, sooner or later we will fail.

Not even the most caring parents can always fulfill their children's needs. Most parents are still untrained in how to properly love and respect their children as human beings, without either spoiling or neglecting them. Other parents are too overwhelmed by work and other duties to provide for their child's emotional needs. Hence, children soon learn that love is only part-time or conditional, and start trying to earn it by striving to be perfect, or at least better than others.

The most common mistakes in child rearing are: exaggerated criticism for a child's mistakes, expecting a child to take responsibility for parent's needs and feelings, and criticizing the child's personality instead of a specific behavior (e.g. "You are so lazy", "This is stupid / ugly", "How can you be so selfish", "Do you want to make Mommy sad"... or even dramatic examples such as I heard from some of my clients: "You are an example of worthlessness", "You are my shit", "I should put you into a sack and drown you like a kitten.").

Very quickly, a child will learn that approval might hopefully be earned by fulfilling exaggerated, often unreasonable or contradictory demands, and that mistakes are not tolerated. The result is an adult who blindly follows even unreasonable rules.

Moreover, some children learn not to trust themselves and their own decisions, if their emotions, conclusions or ideas are often criticized or ridiculed. Thus, as adults, they continue to seek advice and direction from other people, rather than accepting the risk of making a mistake. This creates a more or less subtle dependency on external authority. For this to occur, another aspect of the problem must exist - that of people who place themselves in positions of authority to gain power over others.

These patterns are more obvious with people who join cults or cult-like organizations and fulfill any demands from authorities. On a less dramatic level, similar issues can be observed in all societies. Many people hope that obedient compliance will bring benefits such as love and acceptance, based on experience with parents. The need to be accepted is manifested, for example, in adolescence through obeying and imitating "popular" teenagers, by following trends and fashion or through arbitrary social rules about what is acceptable and what is not. Some rules might make sense, but, just as easily, some might only have made sense decades or even centuries ago.

Many people were taught by their parents to trust authorities. It appears that we have not only emotional, but also genetic needs to follow our parents, needs that guaranteed survival through our evolution. Emotionally, for children it is often too frightening not to trust their parents. Based on their experience with parents, many people tend to trust people who appear to be very confident. They might automatically accept something written in a book or a newspaper without question (although, all the misinformation on the Internet may soon discourage such gullibility). While some power-hungry people want to present their ideas as absolute truths, others might be willing to trust them only because of their confident attitude.

Manipulation and doubt

The greatest damage is often done by subtle manipulators. You can find yourself in situations where everything you hear or read sounds reasonable and correct and it is difficult to find a counter-argument; yet you still feel that something is wrong or missing. My suggestion in such situations is to take a moment to carefully listen to those subtle feelings in your body and try to verbalize them. Information acquired this way often "disarms" people who are trying to manipulate you better than your learned responses.

One way to check if someone is authentic and has good intentions, is to check how that person reacts if you question his or her ideas. Some typical examples of defensive or passive aggressive responses can often be heard in New Age circles. If you opposed someone's theories or requests, you may have been accused of being closed, or of not having enough love, or that you are not "spiritually advanced" enough to understand their ideas, that your "heart (or some other) chakra is closed". Such people will generally attack your personality if you disagree with their ideas. Such responses to your disagreement are often signs of immaturity and inflexibility.

I deeply dislike when abstract, unverifiable theories are presented in detail as absolute truths, such as "there is a spiritual center in (random location) in your body, and to activate it, you have to follow my instructions". This is very common within New Age groups, but not only amongst them.

If we allow for the possibility of being mistaken, we can use expressions like "in my experience" or "it is possible", "I believe" and similar. But if somebody expects you to believe their esoteric ideas, without even questioning if they make sense or how they could be proved, simply because it was claimed by a spiritual book or a 'channeled' authority, detach yourself and be very cautious about such people.

It is wise to accept doubt as a useful and friendly feeling. Without doubts, we could easily be carried away by any theory and become much more vulnerable to manipulation and exploitation. Doubt motivates us to question and differentiate between similar ideas and information. It is quite normal even for scientists, who by definition seek to prove their claims, to have very different and conflicting ideas. They throw away old theories and rigorously check new ones. They may allow their expectations to influence their results. How much easier it is to create theories if our only proof is that "it feels right!".

Listen to your doubts whenever you read a book or talk to someone. Still, be aware that a feeling of resistance can be healthy or unhealthy. Healthy resistance is when you can find realistic reasons for your doubts or disagreements when you examine your feelings; the unhealthy ones are typically irrational. Unhealthy resistance comes from suppressed infantile rebellion against authorities and their demands: for example, children who were forced to behave unselfishly before they were naturally ready to develop that quality, might develop resistance towards any encouragement to be unselfish.

If you notice feelings of resistance, explore which words and idioms trigger them. The difference between healthy and unhealthy resistance can be subtle and sometimes both of them appear simultaneously. Still, you can learn to distinguish between them by practicing observing your emotional reactions.

Do not take anything for granted. Check the information you are given, notice the words and idioms the other person is using. Consider why some claims might be incomplete or misleading. For example, if someone shows you the result of a research study, ask yourself what could have influenced that research to make it insufficiently objective and reliable (don't forget the possibility of the research being paid for by interested parties, as is common practice lately).

We can sound very intelligent even if what we say does not really make sense. Some people who are skillful with words can easily create random combinations of words that sound meaningful, even wise. I have met quite a few such people, and perhaps you have too. For practice, try reading some 'highly intellectual' books, and then explore within your body which words sound to you as carrying a certain depth and which sound like hollow intellectualizing.

One way to manipulate people is to make conclusions from unproven and unreliable statements. Many people will be blinded by the apparent logic of the conclusion and not check the reliability of the "facts" from which they were deduced. Even if the speaker is not consciously lying - how do we to know that his research is accurate? Many people will give you suspicious information with good intentions. Few people seem to closely check the information they spread around.

(It is equally important to check your own behavior, of course. However, since self-examination is included in many other parts of this book, I do not focus on it here and now.)

Manipulators often try to hook you through your ideals and aspirations, using abstract words such as love, light, truth, spirituality, God ... to hide their lack of sincere, sensible arguments.

(A quote from experience: 'You must let your Higher Self show you I'm right!' This is an example of obvious, not very subtle manipulation - skilful manipulators are usually less direct.)

I was once given some good advice, "If somebody talks in big, abstract words, check what he wants from you!" Some people might only want your approval or admiration, while others might want your time, effort or money. Any lack of respect for your personal choices and beliefs, is reason to be cautious, even if you feel that the person might have a point. Another common manipulative tactic is to mix some truth with semi-truths, fabrications and exaggerations. This is commonplace in many religious theories and political speeches.

In everyday human communication, it is rare to hear something that we can accept as a truth without reservation. People talk from their own limiting beliefs, create conclusions on the basis of a small number of examples, selectively adjust facts to their beliefs or to their needs, embellish stories for their own benefit (or just to impress you), accept ideas only because they sound nice or help build their ego. Reality can be twisted in an infinite number of ways, even if unconsciously and unintentionally.

Keep this in mind while talking to people you trust and who you know do not wish to manipulate you. Regardless of how much you appreciate somebody's intelligence, experience, wisdom or spiritual authority, always remember that even that person could make a mistake at any moment. Do not expect anybody to be perfect - simply stay within your own truth and live your own life, instead of somebody else's.

Points to ponder:

Remember people who once represented authority for you (or still do). Remember some beliefs that you used to believe. What made you decide to trust those people or beliefs? Do you like your reasons?

How do you feel about the possibility of following your feelings instead of someone else's?

What kind of approval or attention do you want from your authority figure, and how do you try to achieve it? Are there any similarities between this and your early family?

Do you tend to automatically believe what is written in newspapers or books, or in the results of scientific experiments?

How do you feel when people are particularly self-confident and present their beliefs skillfully and easily?

Practice:

For at least a few days, try to question things other people say, or what you read in different publications. Notice your feelings about doing that, and your approach to determining what is true.

Immature Spirituality

What is the difference between a belief and an illusion? Beliefs are ours; illusions are other people's.

Sometimes, people express their spiritual aspirations by emphasizing strict rules in behavior, "phenomena" (internal images, dreams, coincidences etc.), appearance (while they put real life and relationships in the background), and uncritical acceptance of esoteric theories if they sound good enough (or offer hope for success without much work).

On the other hand, under the surface of nice presentations, one can very often encounter moralizing and intolerance of people with different beliefs and different backgrounds. Those are consequences of a black and white perspective and a lack of understanding and tolerance for other people's experiences.

Let us compare this with the contemporary perception of primitive peoples' beliefs – few people would take their rituals and beliefs seriously today. Perhaps we would interpret some of their ideas in ways that are more fitting to what we know about the world today. In a few hundred years, our descendents may perceive our customs in a similar way – both traditional religions or the New Age experiments.

Many people appear to accept unproven claims out of a desire for acceptance, or out of fear of missing opportunities or provoking authority. Do not be afraid to challenge someone's theories and ask the person to at least explain. Then observe the reaction. People who are honest inwardly and outwardly, would, if nothing else, admit that perhaps there is no proof for their claims, but that they feel comfortable about them and find them reasonable. They would allow your disagreement and let you choose your own beliefs. Other people might be offended or angry – indicating that they are trying to avoid their own doubts, or that they might have some kind of personal advantage from persuading others to trust them.

Some people will accept any esoteric theories, perhaps hoping that their promises would come true, especially if the promises are tempting, or given by authorities or friends. Even recommendations from friends should be taken with a certain amount of precaution, as your friends might be under the influence of temporary good feelings, which can easily be achieved by autosuggestion. A hope for a good result can, by itself, motivate us to avoid questioning a particular belief. Marketers say, "People buy hope, not products!" and that is especially obvious in the marketing of "New Age" products (such as glasses that "energize" water).

I felt attracted to self-improvement work since the age of 15, and I explored all kinds of approaches, sometimes accepting ideas that now seem irrelevant if not without any foundation whatsoever. As I matured, I decided that it is better to learn slowly and gradually, even if I appeared to be "lagging behind" my friends. I wanted to confirm concepts with my own experiences, rather than feel overly excited about new ideas.

Besides, if I cannot confirm something with my own experience, other people's beliefs remain just words for me. The same goes for children and teenagers: people can talk themselves silly trying to warn them or explain some things to them, but often they will only truly understand and will be able to use those lessons, after they have been through a particular experience themselves. On the other hand, other people's experiences do not have to become yours.

People often search for security among like-minded people, or by following rules, trying to earn an authority's approval, or looking for substitutes for parents or other family members. For many, this could be an escape from challenges, troubles and responsibilities, a quest for fast, external solutions. Many young people, just as I was, lack experience, and are more open to trusting authorities or people who appear to have more knowledge and experience. My reason for trusting some of those people was: why would somebody who is otherwise smart, friendly and responsible claim things that were not true? I should at least consider their experience.

I did not, at that time, know enough about self-deceit, auto-suggestion and need to make things feel true, which can make even well-minded people exaggerate and misinterpret their stories. This is also a lesson that needs to be learned, so it makes no sense to urge or criticize people who are in this stage of life.

However, as long as people avoid confronting their own emotions – avoid feeling and embracing them and their messages – and as long as there is intolerance, deliberate misunderstanding, insincerity, self-deceit or power-struggle in their relationships and lives ... no formal spirituality will be of much use. However, the lack of progress might eventually motivate people to explore what is missing in their lives.

Points to ponder:

Consider your spiritual beliefs. Who did you accept them from, and why?

Pretend to represent the opposite opinion, a person who finds arguments against your convictions. How does this feel? Explore your feelings of resistance to this.

New Age and Real Life

Some people feel resistance toward "New Age" ideas and its related terminology simply because they think the movement is stupid by itself. But I think that more people are repelled because many who claim be on a spiritual path, tend to throw around abstract words without sincerity, without true feeling and with a hidden agenda (such as manipulation, criticism, excessive moralizing or subtle bragging).

There is nothing wrong with words like "love", "light", "spirituality", "energy", "personal growth"… but nowadays they are so commonly used in shallow texts and ego-building communication, that they are losing their positive associations and feelings that would normally follow. Instead, more and more people seem to be annoyed by such expressions and associate them with vanity and manipulation.

Lately I have felt that annoyance myself, although there are some texts that can use this terminology without evoking my negative associations. Such texts do not use undue moralizing, nor suggest things such as "ego destruction", "lower Self", "rejecting negativity", or superficial forgiveness. Such writers do not insist on focusing on something or someone outside ourselves, or perceiving God as a personality that is separate from us.

Accepting our own humanity

For me to feel good about particular ideas or publications, the writers need to include acceptance and respect for humanity as a whole and for the challenges of a human life, including all that is often moralistically called "ego", "darkness" or "lower self". Rejection of unpleasant emotions means rejecting parts of ourselves that are not only not "bad" by themselves; they might contain hidden qualities and resources that we have lost or forgotten during difficult times of our lives. The problem is that we have twisted those resources and associated them to fear and toxic beliefs. However, by rejecting, destroying or throwing unpleasant emotions away, all we achieve is to show ourselves that we do not appreciate nor accept our whole personality, no matter how hard we try to convince ourselves of the opposite.

When I say "accept" unpleasant emotions, I do not mean "act them out"! Some people use the idea of accepting all parts of themselves to avoid responsibility for their behavior. You can fully accept yourself with all your current faults, and still be committed and motivated to improve yourself.

Some people still believe in evil, and believe that people are by their nature at least partly evil. If we reject everything within us that is socially unacceptable, we act as if parts of us are evil. Those unhealthy parts of us need healing ... but healing cannot happen if we refuse to notice their signals, if we try to "wash them away" or "burn them" through various energy work, or by prayers to various entities. There is nothing wrong with energy work, if we use it for support when facing our problems, not as an attempt to escape from them.

Looking for external solutions

The critical issue with New Age theories is that many of its followers seem to be seeking external, instant and pleasant solutions to their problems - without having to confront them, learn from them and change their everyday behavior. I was told of a girl who complained to her friend about problems with her boyfriend. She literally told her friend she did not want to work on those issues, but wanted to find "someone who could fix them" (meaning someone who dabbles in "magic"). Many would loudly criticize her example, but many people do similar things in subtle ways. They may call it *energy work* instead of *magic*, and hope that their worldly problems will be carried away.

I also feel that, for many people, the means became the goal: specific methods became goals instead of being tools. Practitioners use such methods to boost their confidence, self-esteem, and often power and status within their groups. Many of them search for skills and experience to feel powerful, or to prove their spiritual progress, emphasizing external appearances instead of internal transformation.

The only proof of our progress is when we gain resources and courage to change our toxic behavioral patterns and make improvements we have avoided. Also, a healthy motivation for change is to feel better internally, instead of "I should" or "this would show my spiritual advancement". To come to that point, you need to accept and explore any resistance to such changes; an attempt to achieve them "overnight" is just another form of self-deceit.

Neglecting personality

Words like "serving" and "humility" are thrown around a lot in the New Age terminology. To me, they feel too much like the old church-imposed ideas of unworthiness and sacrifice, which usually result in hypocrisy. I prefer more moderate expressions such as "help" and "modesty", and I believe that those are much more genuine. Yet most people and most authors of books about spirituality prefer "serving" and "humility", perhaps as a way to feed a "spiritual ego" and show spiritual progress. There is almost no book about spirituality I have read, that has not used those words.

I like the following quote:

"Extreme altruism is no better or nobler than extreme selfishness: both are mistakes. Get rid of the idea that God demands of you to sacrifice yourself for others and that you will assure his help while doing it. Do your best, for yourself and others. You will help more to others while doing your best for yourself than in any other way." (Wallace Wattles)

In other words:

"Do not ask what the world needs, but do what makes your heart sing. Because what the world needs are people with hearts that sing." (Howard Thurman)

The imposed, unbalanced neglect of oneself and focus on others, is one of the things I disagree most with in some New Age approaches. In a similar way, adults may use nice words to manipulate children (such as, "You must love your sister!"), to make them feel bad about themselves and to control them. People who accept such ideas without objections, without checking if they truly feel healthy, may do this out of such childhood conditioning, to prove themselves worthy and please authority.

Once I checked out the second part of a locally popular book by S. N. Lazarev: "The Diagnostics of Karma". While emphasizing an abstract love for God, and an idea that human personality and emotions are secondary, he gives the following example:

The author was sharing a taxi with a friend, and it was his (Lazarev's) turn to pay for the ride. When the ride was over, Lazarev writes, he "felt a sudden urge", jumped out of the taxi and said to his friend, "You pay!". His

150

friend did it without objecting, but afterwards, during a dinner with a group of other people, he started to feel physically sick. Lazarev said to the rest of the group, "I will cure him, but first I have to do one thing" and he whispered in his friend's ear, "You are angry at me because of this taxi thing, ask God to forgive you!" After those words, Lazarev claims, his friend recovered immediately.

The author thought of this as a "funny episode" and a proof of his wisdom. I consider it an "ego-trip" and manipulation, hidden behind big words and ideals. In fact, Lazarev willingly and quite harshly created an obvious imbalance, and then, by a moralistic manipulation, forced his "friend" (who apparently had quite a low self-esteem to start with) to feel ashamed about his natural anger and to suppress it. He actually suppressed it so well, that even his psychosomatic symptoms vanished. (The symptoms might have been an attempt to manipulate from the friend's side too, since he was afraid to show his anger directly). The "healing" could have been a result of the fact that his anger has been noticed, or because he trusted Lazarev, or simple suppression that would later be expressed as self-aggression. I wonder what happened with their friendship and mutual trust afterwards.

Regardless of how we think of God (I definitely do not perceive "him" as some kind of personality separate of us), the fact is that it is much easier, more convenient and less challenging to focus on abstract love for God, than to learn and practice compassion for real people. We create an image of God that suits us, the communication is internal, and the feeling is usually warm and supportive (at least for most people).

Communication with other people is complex and demanding; it takes endless patience, compassion, questioning, balancing our own and other people's needs, courage and sincerity. In the short term, it is much easier and more appealing to turn to an inner image of God instead. But is this crucial for our growth and progress? If, at the same time, no work is done with emotions and relationships, then I claim it is not. True change requires true challenges, decisions and action. There is more opportunity to practice spirituality through conscious, responsible living in the material world, than in all the abstract philosophy in the Earth.

Points to ponder:

Do you try to always be perfect and follow high ideals like serving and humility?

How do you hope the other people would perceive you, if you act like that? How you hope to feel about yourself?

How do you feel in moments when you fail to follow your ideals through?

Do you hope for some external benefits, if you fulfill particular moral criteria?

If you practice a particular spiritual path, what is your opinion about people who choose other paths?

What results do you hope to get from the methods you use? Is it possible that you might be trying to avoid challenges and risks in the outer world?

Emotions and Energy Work

The motivation to write this chapter came through a conversation with a lady who claimed that my thesis that emotional problems are the most common cause of life's blocks was 'completely wrong, unproven and illogical'. She said that "techniques of emotional healing are *passé*", and that she preferred approaches that attempted to resolve "influences of external energies".

In the same week, I read in several books and articles ideas that unwanted emotions and beliefs are just consequences of energy blocks. This is comparable to a scientific concept that emotions are caused by the flow of chemicals through our neurological system, and not the other way around. This sounds like a 'tail wags the dog' theory to me.

I notice that many people favor the idea that their emotional issues are caused by things that they cannot influence (such as astrology or karma), or by something that they hope to influence externally (such as using crystals, rearranging furniture, energy work ...). I see this as attempts to avoid responsibility and confrontation with difficult, unpleasant emotions.

I wish to express my opinion, and I do not expect anyone to agree with me without questioning. My experience is that sometimes only through listening to all emotions, even the unpleasant ones, can we recognize the messages that come from deeper parts of us. In this way can we recognize many hidden and subtle ways in which we neglect ourselves and our needs and fail to express ourselves. We might be surprised to realize how strongly we perceive such behavior as natural, and justify other people's neglect. In the same way, unpleasant feelings also warn us when we consider behaving in unhealthy or egotistic ways. Learning to recognize subtle abuse and neglect, of either ourselves or other people, is easiest if we acknowledge our emotions and listen to them.

At a more spiritual level, unpleasant emotions warn us about the areas in which our lives do not reflect our true being, or in which we avoid learning our "lessons". If not unpleasant emotions, what else could give us such quick, obvious and direct reminders? Unpleasant emotions show us a lot about what do we need to learn.

If we ignore our emotions, our next reminders may come as medical symptoms or a life crisis. In my experience, the more I learn to listen to my emotions "on the spot", when they are still mild, the more I learn from moderate and light situations, and the less I attract intense external problems or experience emotional crises. More and more, I can listen and learn from emotions that come up in situations that could be called healthy or normal. ("Normal" does not always mean "healthy"!)

Becoming aware, accepting and listening to emotions, is, in my experience, the fastest and the most powerful way to love yourself. This attitude confirms to our inner child that we are acceptable and that our needs and internal messages are important.

Saying that emotions are caused by outside, uncontrollable influences and trying to resolve them through external remedies, seems like claiming that we are powerless and robotic, primarily controlled by environmental circumstances rather than by our own minds. If I believed in this, I would lose my sense of meaning of life, as well as motivation to improve myself.

According to Martyn Carruthers, spirituality has been, for a long time, dominated by male principles, while female principles have been largely rejected. Spiritual teachers have been teaching intellectual ideas about enlightenment, implying that we should separate ourselves from experiences and emotions; that we should have empty minds and be indifferent toward our social and physical environment. I believe that this may be a stage in spiritual growth, but true spirituality should include connectedness, joy, creativity and fulfilling relationships. For me, spirituality is more of an experience of fullness rather than emptiness.

"Negative" Emotions

"Negative" emotions that are so condemned in New Age circles are as important as "positive" emotions. Every emotion gives us an important message: anger, for example, is an attempt to defend ourselves, other people or values that are important to us; fear warns us of some kind of danger; sadness sends us a message about what is really important to us, and yet missing in our lives; jealousy is doubt in our own worth, and so on.

Most unpleasant emotions, if they are childish and black and white, indicate toxic beliefs that imply rejection of a part of our true being. For example, childish guilt might indicate a belief that "something is wrong with me" which means that we had to give up something – our sense of self-worth, trust in our instincts, spontaneity, openness or similar – to create such a belief. To bring back those parts of who we truly are, the easiest and the most basic way is to confront our emotions and explore them. Think of all emotions, especially the stronger ones, as markings on a treasure map.

There is no such thing as negative emotion. Instead of dividing emotions into positive and negative, I prefer to use the terms "pleasant" and "unpleasant" emotions. Unpleasant emotions are as natural, honest and important as the pleasant ones, and should be treated with the same attention and appreciation.

Many people think that exploring unpleasant emotions is like "digging through rubbish" and claim it is unnecessary. This can be true if we have heard the message of a particular emotion and truly recognized and learned what we could from it. In that case, the emotions will clear out spontaneously anyway. Yet, much more often, such statements seem to be expressing an intent to *get rid* of unpleasant emotions as fast and as easily as possible. Yet how can we change something that we are not aware of, nor in contact with?

However, people who learn to listen to and explore their feelings risk identifying with, or "immersing" themselves into unpleasant emotions. People who let unpleasant emotions take over may put themselves into victim roles, and some may even enjoy their suffering. I do not recommend fixating on unpleasant emotions. It is better to keep a basically positive attitude, while being aware of and open to the messages that come from unpleasant emotions, accepting them when they spontaneously appear. It is a "shortcut", maybe a steep one, to a much faster path of personal development.

Points to ponder:

How do you feel about promises that particular, "special" people can solve your problems; or that relocating your furniture, placing crystals, using symbols etc – will quickly, dramatically and permanently change your life?

Do you appreciate all your emotions? If not, why not?

Practice:

Observe yourself in situations when you feel intense unpleasant emotions. Try to accept them and fully experience them; listen to their messages.

Do you find that you stop yourself from experiencing unpleasant emotions? What can you do about this?

Practical Action and Continuous Self-Improvement

An old saying tells us that "the best things in life are free", and many people behave as if this was their guiding principle. We wait for perfect partners with whom the rest of our lives would be ecstasy without any trouble. We expect that in a true friendship, misunderstandings, disagreements and imperfections never happen. We hope that somehow we will make a lot of money while sitting at home doing nothing ... and we wish for extraordinary experiences to happen overnight. Often, we use the above mentioned saying in hope to get more than we are willing to give.

If we wish to reach the top of the Himalayas, we could do it by taking a helicopter ride. We would see the results right away – but nothing would change on the inside. There would be nothing that we could call success, no experience to enrich us, to make us more complete. There would be no challenges to overcome. And if life would bring us in front of even the smallest mountain, we would have no knowledge, no preparedness and no more courage than before.

Or we could try to climb it in just one day. Most likely, we would give up after a short while, exhausted and disappointed, and maybe conclude that climbing a mountain does not make much sense at all.

Or we could learn and become aware of the challenges in front of us, research and equip ourselves with all the tools needed to make our climbing easier – and be willing to do the work ourselves. We know that there are many people who will never attempt this climb. We know that the majority would give up and that some might even die while trying to reach the top. If we are willing to take the risk, then we can choose to travel in a slow pace, stopping along the way to admire all the views and fully examine all parts of the road. Or we can take a steeper but faster road, along with bigger challenges, more intense experiences that will build both our strength and endurance. Neither of those two roads are better or worse, they are just two different paths to choose from.

Once we reach the top, there is so much more there than just a spectacular view. We know that the success is ours and that we have learned what we might need in the future, if we ever face a similar challenge. We are aware of our abilities and strengths acquired through all the challenges along the way. We might have confronted difficult decisions, sometimes turned the wrong way, kept going even in moments when we felt that there was no more strength left in us for the next step – but this is exactly how we built our strength, step by step. We are now different people then when we first started our journey. We became more complete human beings, enriched by many moving, intense experiences, which we might afterwards remember even with a bit of nostalgia.

Love, friendship, success are never for free. The initial feeling of deep infatuation is useful as a "tester", but to build true love and intimacy, we have to be ready for a long-term investment and confrontation with many challenges. However, I do not claim that effort is valuable all by itself (as if filling a bottomless bucket with water, over and over again, and then bragging about how hard we worked). The value is in learning, in the strength, joy and experience that follow as a result. We can focus on difficulties and troubles – or we can focus on the depth of the feeling, intensity of the experience and richness of the final result.

Experiencing life intensely and accepting all of our emotions can help us to live more in the present moment. It might seem as if time flows in a different rhythm, since it is full of experience (to me it feels that, in emotionally intense periods, time slows down, like while being on a journey, but some people claim the opposite). This richness is built out of pleasant and unpleasant emotions. A common ideal in many New Age philosophies is that people who work on their personal development should overcome emotions like fear, sadness, anger... should look at everything with a smile or indifference and approach every experience with positive attitude. I think this is neither healthy nor motivating. Sometimes sadness can be a good reminder about how important love is, fear or doubt can motivate great courage and change, and anger is a great motivator to stand up for ourselves and our values.

Implementing changes

Most people start working on self-improvement with a desire for results to occur overnight and focus on external rather than internal change. Advertising messages encourage them enthusiastically in that direction (few marketers profit if people actually solve their problems!). Many people hope that, using some technique, they can create a new sense of self without risking (sometimes scary) specific actions in daily life, e.g., telling someone what bothers you or what you want, finding a better job or building a business... If you perceive such actions as too difficult or too unpleasant, it usually means that you do not yet have enough motivation to change or - more commonly - that you have not yet achieved real internal change.

External life experiences deeply influence our subconscious and can be a test on whether we have really learned our specific life lessons or not. One could say that, if we could do it all in our heads, there would be no purpose for living in the physical world. The blessing we often gain through difficulties is that the physical world uncompromisingly forces us onto the path of growth, often through difficult and demanding challenges, which, sooner or later, we cannot avoid or turn our heads away from.

We can choose whether we will accept a worthwhile challenge, or feel sorry for ourselves, claiming that life is too difficult to deal with. In the first case, your life may not become easier - especially in the beginning - because you will need to come to terms with a number of situations, decisions and choices that you may have previously tried to avoid or postpone. However, the wealth of experience, the intensity of living your life fully, and increased trust and respect for yourself, are pleasures for which abandoning the path of least resistance is a very low price to pay.

For example, many people hope that people would treat them differently if they do enough meditation, visualization etc. They hope that if they "radiate differently" or feel better with themselves, people will automatically adapt or nicer experiences will "come their way". In some cases, people might pick up on our different non-verbal signals and feel when we are stronger. However, more often, people around us will not change much. This is a challenge, as well as an opportunity, to confront others in honest communication, and to face the fears that might come with those scarier and riskier choices.

My personal experience is that when I firmly decide to overcome my inhibitions and tell other people what I have been avoiding to express for a long time, they may spontaneously change their attitude towards me even before the confrontation. I must emphasize that this occurs only if I am fully willing to take that risk. Still, in most situations, especially in the case of long term and important relationships, this is not enough. You will likely need to invest effort, uncover your deepest and not very logical needs and beliefs, and risk misunderstanding and conflict. In such a way, we grow as human beings and create closeness, understanding and love for self and others.

Sometimes, people might be aware that they are not ready for new ways of thinking, for the adjustments and risks that might follow if they would change their limiting beliefs. As one of my clients said, it might bring too much energy and freedom, she would have to start focusing on her goals and take responsibility for her life – which can be frightening and carry risks of guilt and failure. It is everyone's right to progress at the pace that suits him or her. You might want to give yourself some time before jumping into deep water, or make foundations before building the walls. It is also a good idea to explore the roots of your fears: how did you learn that responsibility is a burden, or that having your own goals means feeling guilty?

There is no technique that would be a magic wand and a shield from life challenges. In my experience, methods that promise such things reflect dishonest marketing, self-delusion or short term placebo-effects. Methods such as Soulwork Systemic Coaching, that focus on the roots of the problems, can help you resolve emotional and mental blocks and build new self-image, trust, motivation and awareness of our strengths. Yet developing new habits and actively achieving our goals require full commitment. More and more, I feel how important practical action is in completing any self-improvement effort. Without doing that, we would never truly know whether or not we have changed, or if we in fact only thought about changing.

Money and Creativity

Money is one of the areas linked to most fears, guilt and struggle. Some people feel that their work is never good enough to justify being paid or asking for a fair price. That belief makes them waste a lot of their time and energy to make hardly enough money to cover their basic needs, which blocks their overall progress in self-improvement.

Once we learn to create financial security, a wider spectrum of areas of learning and challenges opens to us, areas that, until that point, we had no time to explore. Think about what you would really like to do, if you already had enough financial means. What would your interests be, your new desires, and what new fields of study would you focus on? One of my friends said that he realized while still a student that if he would work on jobs provided by others, he would only have enough for basic survival. So he built his own business, and now that the business practically runs itself, he focuses on what he is most passionate about – teaching people parenting skills.

Guilt and helplessness

Guilt about money is partly due to the fact that many people obtain and use money in a selfish manner. Selfishness is partly based on biological urges for power and domination, but mostly on childish feelings of "I am not good enough as I am – I have to prove my worth". People who feel balanced inside and who respect themselves, do not need to constantly prove themselves nor hoard more, more and more. Weight, for anorexic people, slowly becomes an obsessive focus and a measure of their personal worth and qualities. Some people have a similar attitude about money. Their parents probably valued money more than their own children.

On the other hand, a toxic self-image can stimulate unconscious sabotage of financial success. If, subconsciously, we do not believe that we are worthy enough, we might not allow ourselves to be successful. We will find, without even noticing, all kinds of ways to sabotage or destroy potential big achievements.

Our material wishes may trigger subtle guilt and anxiety. A belief that we cannot fulfill such wishes usually originates in early childhood. Once we learn to focus on the essence of a desire, instead of superficial sense of guilt or fear, the desire can become a source of motivation and creative energy, a powerful impulse that will push us toward its achievement.

Growing through creativity

Many people hope to obtain money without investing much effort. If you have learned not to take initiative nor trust your own abilities, you might be tempted to turn to esoteric approaches hoping to create money "out of the blue". Although optimism is important, it cannot replace involvement in the physical life, creativity, learning and improving your skills, or contributing to other people's lives in exchange for what you receive.

In his book "Rich Dad, Poor Dad", Robert Kiyosaki recognizes a significant fact: our educational system teaches and prepares children to look for jobs offered by others, instead of encouraging entrepreneurship and creativity. Fortunately, more and more people are becoming aware that it is not only inefficient, but also unwise to rely on others to create jobs and income, often in unpleasant working environments and with salaries that hardly enable plain survival. More and more people develop and use their creativity to offer unique and recognizable products and services (sometimes a bit too unique). Perhaps in time, step by step, our society could change from focusing on survival and basic safety into the world of freedom and creativity – a world full of people who create their own professions instead of only choosing from the existing jobs.

No one in history who ever created something truly valuable did it overnight. Biographies of extraordinary people tell us stories of commitment, endurance, dedicated search for new knowledge and solutions, and often about challenging life conditions and risky decisions, too.

When people achieve superficial material success without particular effort, very often many emotional and social problems and immature behaviors follow. This seems true for many movie stars and children of wealthy parents. Hard work and effort have little value by themselves (although some people believe that they would earn happiness if they suffer enough!); the value of work is in acquiring knowledge, developing skills and creativity, resolving problems, confronting risks and building endurance. People who became rich suddenly or without their own merit, may lack the qualities gained by confronting challenges.

To become masters of our own lives, we need to develop through many experiences and challenges, many different situations, even by repeatedly approaching similar challenges using a variety of strategies. This is as true for financial abundance as for partnership, parenthood, friendship or spirituality. We all love to daydream about fast solutions for our problems and "living happily ever after", but this is not realistic. Besides, it would be boring. Challenges, emotional intensity and joy through everyday insights and discoveries enhance passion for life. Add to this the satisfaction of looking back and realizing how much we have achieved. Perhaps this passion for life is what many people who became rich effortlessly miss in their lives, as well as self-esteem and compassion for others. Neither status symbols nor money can replace that.

In my workshops on creative learning, I emphasize exercises that involve emotional and intellectual engagement, creativity, games that motivate learning and interlinking knowledge. However, I notice that many people – even children – usually write one or two short ideas and then passively wait for the exercise to finish.

Unfortunately, I am quite certain that their lives will follow a similar pattern: passive anticipation of instant solutions, accepting "a path of least resistance" with minimal emotional and creative involvement. A gloomy life full of routine that I do not wish on anyone.

The activities of mass media seem designed to deliberately numb young people down, transforming them into consumer robots focused on appearance and shopping. Whether you believe or not that certain groups do this on purpose, this is the result: young people who, on one hand, wish to avoid activity and effort, and on the other wish to get rich quickly so that they can buy status symbols. This leads to their acceptance of and participation in silly media activities, and the vicious circle continues.

Probably not everything is so dark – compared to past centuries, possibilities and horizons are much wider, and besides the choice of being passive, there are many more possibilities on the creative and active side of life. I meet many young people who are motivated and aware of the immaturity of our civilization, who are eager to reflect more deeply, to be creative and to get into action.

Few people can be truly creative or eager to learn more about subjects that do not attract them. They will most likely focus only on results, while disliking the process of achieving them. You are unlikely to achieve success while doing something you do not enjoy, something that you only do with "half a heart". In today's world, full of both opportunities and harsh competition, to create real and long-term success, you must be truly an expert in what you do.

Quality follows spontaneously, even without you noticing, if you enjoy researching and reflecting about your work, if it is important to you to gain more than just knowledge, if the search for answers is something you find important, not just something that brings financial results. At that point, work is not just work in your mind, it is your way of life, an important topic of your everyday thoughts. You may even get out of bed in the middle of the night just to write down an idea, which bubbled up while you were lying in bed relaxed. If your interest and knowledge about a particular profession are average, you are likely to achieve average results as well.

Taking responsibility

A crucial and common cause of money problems is perceiving other people or society as the source of money, instead of realizing that it is ourselves and our efforts. Just as with love, this can lead to dependence, possessiveness, unrealistic expectations, manipulation or other unhealthy attempts to gain what we want. Or we can give up and reject opportunities.

If we perceive other people as being responsible for our poor financial situation, we might avoid paying for their work, or might even cheat them using different excuses. Some scams like fare-dodging in public transport and internet "pirating" have become almost normal and everyone has their own justifications. Justifications usually include one's own financial situation, which is rejection of personal responsibility. If we feel dependent on others as a source of money, we might often complain about their prices, while on the other hand setting high prices for our own services. We want others to be aware of the time and costs we invest in our products, while at the same time neglecting and ignoring their work and their needs.

The belief that we are financially dependent on other people often

164

includes the idea that others depend on us too – with consequent guilt if we ask for compensation for our work. Similarly, we might also feel that we lose if we have to pay for something. Then money may become a source of frustration and immature behavior, instead of being perceived as a system of exchange.

Just like the majority of our expectations, beliefs and problems, we develop our relationship with money in our early years. That relationship starts with feeling dependent on our parents. Our expectations then intensify or modify, depending on our parent's beliefs and behavior in relation to money.

Children are naturally demanding and ask for a lot. They want to see and try everything, they want to enjoy opportunities and they are not aware that some are not so readily available. A great deal of media marketing targets children, since the advertising industry knows how urgent children's desires are, how prone they are to external influence and how little they can postpone or deny themselves pleasure.

It is up to parents to cope with such demands and to explain to their children about how money works. Parents who see their source of money in the hands of others, will teach such ideas to their children, and will often teach children to feel guilty if they ask for something. They may also convey the idea that money is something bad.

Calling money "bad" brings forth the very problems that it tries to avoid: hypocrisy, unspoken expectations, avoidance and manipulation. It is a similar attitude as people had towards sexuality in the past: blaming and condemning healthy pleasure instead of recognizing unhealthy selfishness and eliminating violence.

If parents measure one's worth in money, while at the same time criticize children for having desires, children are in conflict. They are likely to create (and suppress) fears, guilt and anger. They might attempt to end their confusion by using double standards to justify greedy and unhealthy behaviors that result from their frustrations. Many people use ideas such as "It's their fault if they are stupid and naive enough to believe my lies", or "Survival of the fittest" to justify deception and ruthlessness on individual or global scale.

Instead, we can teach children to earn and enjoy money, but not identify with it. If children learn to value themselves over their bank accounts, they are more likely to value other people that way too, and to consider ethical behavior, especially in business. This includes adequate salaries for all workers (not just upper management), environmental and health concerns, human working conditions and contributing to social causes. If you have children and you are frustrated with their requests, do not blame them - teach them to save, prioritize and choose wisely, and to create goods and services that they can exchange for what they want.

Points to ponder:

How do you feel about your material wishes? Do you feel guilty, frustrated, discouraged or angry? Do you blame others for not fulfilling them?

Do you truly enjoy what you do? If not, how do you feel when you consider changing that situation?

How do you feel when you are asked for money? How do you feel when you need to ask for money?

Do you believe that your "net worth" defines you (or other people)?

Developing Creativity

Creativity is not a random gift given to lucky individuals. Creativity is a skill that can be practiced and developed. Einstein is quoted for saying: *"It's not that I'm so smart, it's just that I stay with problems longer!"*

Just like driving a bicycle, playing a musical instrument, reading ... creativity can be learned and perfected. It is important to understand that, just as with these skills, it is necessary to invest time, perseverance and interest. As children, we naturally accept that we still need to learn many things, we feel enthusiastic about learning and we put effort into it. As adults with many obligations, we may lack patience or energy for investing time and effort into developing yet another skill.

Skills are activities that require learning and effort. With frequent repetition, they can become automatic. Repeated behaviors tend to become automatic, so that more brain capacity can be redirected towards other things. Anything we repeat regularly, either desired skills or unwanted habits, creates connections between neurons in our brain, which facilitate learning so that new actions become easier and more automatic with time.

Just as drivers automatically change gears or press brakes in a car, we may, in certain situations, automatically do what we have often done before. We might frequently, even when a habit is unwanted such as smoking, move to light a cigarette semi-automatically, almost as if we were not aware of our movements. Thus we can create a habit of eating under stress, or turning on a TV, or sitting by a computer to kill what little free time we have left... and in turn disregard our habitual thoughts and emotions.

If you pay attention, you may notice that your thoughts follow specific patterns depending on the topics in your mind. Those patterns are also habits, neurologically reinforced ways of thinking, created by frequent repetition. To develop creativity, we can work to make a habit of a somewhat more difficult and more complex way of functioning – thinking outside of boxes, outside of automatism, creating new, non-routine thoughts, frequently through interlinking quite unrelated ideas and information.

This sounds like a paradox: attempting to create an automatic habit of avoiding automatic thinking habits. Maybe it is better to describe it as creating a habit of consciously paying attention to your thoughts and nudging them in unexpected directions, encouraging associations that we would not normally make.

Lateral thinking may never become fully automatic - to create something new, conscious and active participation is needed - however, we can train our brain to do it easier, faster and more efficiently. In short: we cannot create a habit of automatically forming new ideas, but we can create a habit of nudging our thoughts *towards* new ideas.

Like intelligence, the process of creative thinking is most efficient in the fields in which we invest most of our time and interest. However, once acquired, such ways of thinking can yield results in other fields as well, although perhaps less frequently and efficiently. Famous creative people - Einstein, Tesla, numerous artists - had one or few fields in which they were the most creative - areas which attracted them, interested them, and involved them emotionally; which they enjoyed pondering and in which they enjoyed investing their time. But at the same time, this made it easier for them to think outside the box in other fields beside their main areas of interest, and to be more creative than people with routine thinking habits.

Apart from creative thinking habits, creativity often requires knowledge. You need to be familiar with details of the area in which you want to develop something new. One simple and excellent definition says: an idea is old information rearranged in a new way. In order to rearrange knowledge, we first have to have it - we have to be familiar with the field in which we want to employ our creativity. Obviously, it is not realistic to expect, for example, a physicist to be particularly creative in psychotherapy or vice versa. However, some especially valuable creative achievements have been achieved by interlinking different disciplines, like J. S. Bach who used mathematics to create music. However, in those cases the authors had knowledge and interest in both fields, they did not choose them randomly.

Nowadays, one needs a lot of knowledge to be creative, considering the current pace of new ideas and information being created throughout the world. To gather this knowledge, we need time, motivation and interest. We can be most creative in the fields we think about a lot, in which we enjoy investing time, about which acquiring knowledge is not duty, but pleasure.

Motivation, interest and enjoyment in the process itself are crucial to develop any skill. If you do something with only results in mind (like a weight reduction diet), but you do not find the process of achieving that goal enjoyable, it is just another obligation. Your focus would then be much weaker and you would easily find excuses for avoiding and postponing action. You will likely invest only as much effort as you have to, or as much as you force yourself to. This is why finding ways in which practicing creativity can be pleasant and enjoyable, is crucial for success.

Humor can be one of those ways. Humor is closely linked to creativity since it is based on unexpected associations. A witty twist in a sentence or a story requires an ability to think on several levels quickly; what you say must make sense, and perhaps have a hidden meaning or several meanings, and at the same time it must be unexpected and even absurd. Exceptionally creative people are often funny and vice versa.

Have you read a funny book or seen a comedy, then noticed that your brain spontaneously continued to think along that similar style? Perhaps you were more likely to notice possible funny twists in your surroundings, in conversations around you, or in your own thoughts? If you do not consciously persevere in this way of thinking, after some time you will fall back to your normal thinking habits.

Witty people are an example of trained creativity: they did not create such thinking habits overnight. They have trained their brains to reach beyond the boundaries of the logical and expected, to actively link ideas in unexpected ways that do not have to be perfect and correct.

Being willing to sometimes think in illogical and weird ways, is exceptionally important for the creative process. Considering works of art or scientific achievements, the world sees only the finished results. It does not see the time, trials, mistakes, and numerous corrections that preceded it. It is easy to create an impression that great achievements are products of particularly inspired moments, which an average individual could never achieve. But it is rarely true.

Creativity requires our willingness to make mistakes before we achieve success, to explore different directions, which will often appear to be "in vain", to create numerous ideas, of which only a small number are applicable.

Pay attention to how you feel about your ideas and what you expect from them. Consider how you evaluate and discard your ideas, as well as how you feel when you are not successful in creating a useful new idea within a desired time or of a desired quality.

Discarding ideas is one more consequence of a common need to be perfect and "the best". Most people will automatically discard all ideas, which do not appear impressive enough, even before giving them proper thought. When we allow ourselves to consider ideas that might not be the most splendid, and think how we can eliminate their drawbacks, very often such ideas can prove to be steps towards better ones.

Another reason for rejecting ideas is distrust in one's own abilities . Most people from time to time have ideas with lots of potential. However, most people will not pursue those ideas due to fear, lack of confidence or lack of motivation. In such cases, we usually find excuses such as, "*It would be too much work*" or, "*I am too old ... have no time ... have no money ...* " etc., even if our ideas could change our lives for the better. If you find yourself doing this, hold on to your ideas a little longer, just for the experiment's sake, and think how the mentioned obstacles could be removed or how you could use at least a part of your ideas. Maybe you will get more ideas in this process!

Creativity is systematically, although perhaps not intentionally, discouraged in most children. Many parents feel the need to constantly correct their children. They might be driven by habit, or by a desire to impart as much knowledge as possible to their children, but sometimes also by their conditioned fear of their child challenging traditions and accepted beliefs and thus attracting public displeasure. Also, some parents have an immature need for their children to be special and better than others - such parents hope to prove their own worth to other people.

Even if these limiting habits are not present, few parents know how to encourage and stimulate their children to create ideas, and fewer still are willing to join their children and participate in this process. Most of us were brought up to give expected answers, not to stick out too much and to perform our tasks automatically. So we often end up teaching our children the same patterns, although perhaps with good intentions.

Even so, a family environment can allow much more freedom and creativity than school. Our school system seems to be almost designed to hamper children's thinking and curiosity, to make children fit into rigid frames and to deliver them to factories that need workers. Putting children in concrete boxes, in which they must follow strict schedules every day for twelve or more years of their lives, feels more like training animals than raising children to live good lives.

A strict schedule is just the beginning. Next, children are conditioned to behave and think in a uniform manner. They are punished not only for spontaneous behavior, which must be strictly controlled, but also for responses that are not classed as correct. Even in more creative activities such as essay writing or visual arts, children are frequently discouraged to follow their ideas if their ways of thinking are not to the teacher's taste. Naturally, this depends on a teacher's personality, but since even the best teachers are still emotionally conditioned humans, they will unconsciously mold children through their systems of incentives and punishments. I remember my sister complaining that every time she wrote an essay that truly represented her points of view, she would get a C, while every time she wrote what she knew the teacher expected, she would get an A.

Such educational systems are under pressure from more liberal upbringing and media, which offer behavior models quite different to those expected in schools. However, governments still need employees who will work eight hours a day doing whatever they are told to do, so things are not likely to change soon. It remains to be seen how this will develop (and how concerned parents can change educational systems).

To develop creativity, it is equally important to have conscious focus as well as to build awareness of your internal processes and to perceive and translate these in words to the best of your ability. Creativity is not a rational process. You can initiate it rationally, giving your mind information and an intention to create new ideas. However, this will seldom suffice. Important ideas most frequently come in form of sudden insights, the well known "aha" effect, preceded by a period of unconscious data processing. The "aha" effect is achieved more easily during those moments when we are in a closer contact with our inner world, feelings and subconscious. This is why we can frequently read anecdotes about famous people searching inspiration in various rituals, which primarily served to relax them and redirect their attention from rational thinking. Some people say that they come up with their best ideas during walks, while relaxing in a bath, during meditation, immediately before or after sleeping, or even within dreams.

The more aware you are of your emotions, the more easily you will recognize and verbalize subconscious impulses, sometimes very subtle and of short duration. This ability is a basis of creativity. Many people need practice to become deeply aware of their feelings. If we have (and most people have) spent a large part of our lives controlling and suppressing emotions, our ability to feel them can be "underdeveloped". This shows differently in different people, depending on how much, and in which context, they learned as children to suppress their emotions. However, when working with people, I notice that a considerable number of people have problems perceiving any other detail apart from naming an emotion; in rare cases they find it difficult even to name their emotions.

Give yourself time! Many people give up quickly after their first two or three ideas do not please them. Through experience, I have found out that I usually need two to three days of intense focus on a problem for my subconscious to actively work on it and generate quality ideas.

Just start! Creativity comes only through action, never through waiting for something to happen and for an idea to come "on a silver plate". This will almost never happen. Sometimes taking a piece of paper and letting your thoughts flow, can have unexpected results. It is interesting that for many people a deadline (close to running out) encourages speed and quality of creating ideas. This is as if we sent a message to our subconscious, "This is truly important!" and it cooperates. On the other hand, some people find that a sense of urgency is too stressful for them and could diminish their performance.

In short, going beyond our usual cognitive processes, as well as exploring unusual associations and ideas, represent a basis for creative thinking. A crucial part of this process is to accept ideas and associations that at first do not necessarily seem realistic or logical. We could call this an *inter-idea*. Next, departing from that point, we allow new trains of thought in the direction of analyzing and improving the *inter-idea,* which may eventually lead to a completely different, but quality solution.

Emotional Health and Relationship with the Body

Food as an Addiction

A healthy psyche requires a healthy body. Chemical and hormonal imbalances influence our emotions, even if this might not be easy to recognize. Therefore, I decided to include the topic in this book, although it might appear tangential at first glance.

Too many theories and rules have appeared lately concerning nutrition. As a result, many people are confused, while some, discouraged, give up and return to their customary, unconscious and unhealthy eating habits. As in other areas of life, my approach to food is to avoid too many petty rules and follow some simple, general principles that sound logical to me. A crucial one, as far as food is concerned, is that it is prudent to eat the most natural and fresh food available and to avoid processed foods. Most people choose to ignore this, because they do not want to give up the products they are used to. Also, it appears that not caring about your health is considered "masculine" in patriarchal mentalities.

Cardiovascular diseases are the result of unhealthy eating habits and are the primary causes of death in western societies. Besides, more and more people suffer fairly early in life from degenerative diseases. A common one, and often dreaded, is cellulite, but I also know quite a few young people, even students, who suffer from chronic diseases and pathological processes in their bodies, even though they are slim and do not overeat.

We are an addiction-obsessed civilization. We use every possible method or activity to draw our attention away from our true feelings and needs. Anything that can temporarily divert our focus from ourselves, can be addictive: from certain habitual daily activities, to heavy psychoactive drugs. Processed food is one of the most common and most subtle addictions: neither the effects of poor quality food, nor the symptoms of addictive behavior are intense and obvious in the short term .

One reason is that, at a very early age, we associated food with love and emotional pleasure. For babies, nursing is often the highest pleasure; it is associated with closeness, caressing and safety. Older children, facing frustrations, prohibitions and criticism, usually find relief in being reminded of that earlier pleasure. At a deep level, we perceive the food we were given at an early age as having emotional value, which makes it psychologically attractive. A Croatian man who emigrated and now owns a restaurant in the USA, wrote on his blog that American people are so used to canned and processed food, that a meal made from scratch does not evoke nostalgic, "home-made-food" feelings as much as supermarket-bought food.

Since many parents have only shallow ideas about nutrition, children are commonly given unnatural, processed food full of sugar and chemicals (and advertised as "healthy"). This builds a basis for addictions. Growing children are commonly offered candies as expressions of love, reward or as a distraction. Consequently, as adults we continue to use such food for the same purposes, for ourselves and our children. Most people seem to care more about the cleanliness and efficiency of their cars than of their own bodies.

Apart from chemical addictions, processed food causes emotional addictions, too. From an early age certain foods, because of their pleasant taste and their stimulation of endorphins, are associated with emotional satisfaction and stress relief. Many people are familiar with the longing for sweets or other foods during times of stress, or simply for achieving emotional fulfillment. Many people even believe that such longings are healthy and natural. (Why do we almost never long for carrots or kale?)

Where milder levels of addiction are concerned, moderate consumption of foods that we long for can achieve the desired effect; however, with stronger emotions and deeper emotional voids, not even large amounts of food can satisfy our emotional needs, only dull them somewhat. For different reasons, however, we often act as though we were too lazy to deal with those emotions. As a consequence, not only do we ingest more and more toxins, we also miss the possibility of healing our emotions and learning to create joy and fulfillment in spontaneous and natural ways.

In fact, even if we resolve our chemical addiction by controlling our urges, emotional needs that we do not satisfy in healthy ways will quickly stimulate us to return to such foods, or to shift to another addiction. It is an illusion to hope that emotional addiction can be resolved through

174

willpower alone. Emotions cannot be resolved through suppression and rejection, especially not those emotions that are strong enough to stimulate us to become addicts. The more we suppress them, the more we strengthen them. This is one reason why most diets and other addiction treatment methods fail.

Overeating

Most people treat their bodies like trash cans. We may stuff food into ourselves out of habit, emotional needs or ideas (e.g. "*It's a sin to throw food away*"), instead of listening to our bodies. Afterwards, we wonder where our cellulite comes from and why we cannot get rid of it, while considering degenerative processes to be coincidences or normal consequences of aging.

People are ready to pay for pharmaceutical products that promise higher levels of energy and vitality, while at the same time regularly diminishing their energy with unhealthy food and lifestyle. Why pay for artificial energy, when a healthy diet has so many advantages: physical vitality, higher level of emotional balance (although a healthy diet cannot solve emotional problems by itself!) and feeling good in our bodies – and we waste less money too!

Many people believe that healthy food is expensive and tastes bland. This is a commercially fabricated illusion. Industries have recognized the growing desire of people to take care of their diet, so they try to convince us that we should buy expensive products if we want high quality and taste. Many products advertised as healthy are highly processed and deprived of nutrients.

I think it is normal to enjoy mild, subtle, yet rich tastes of natural food, but many people do not have a chance to develop such a taste. One of my friends is quite hedonistic - she enjoys food and has no desire whatsoever to deny herself that pleasure. However, when she, as an experiment, decided to eat mainly fresh and light food for a while, she noted that her taste changed within a few weeks, and she was less and less attracted to low quality, processed food. It is important to note, though, that despite her hedonism, she was not addicted to particular foods in the first place; an addiction would have slowed her progress and would have made it more difficult for her to change.

Social customs and expectations make it even harder to avoid poor quality food. Besides, along with advertisers that try to reinforce our unhealthy urges, emotional longings for specific products often make people believe that they need them. This is a possible danger of the idea of following your body: you might find yourself following your unhealthy needs. Just like emotions, healthy physical urges are more subtle and less urgent than unhealthy ones.

Science in service of corporate profit

Nutrition has become a corporate battlefield. There are more and more books and articles that try to make us avoid certain types of food (even if unprocessed), even whole groups of foods, while emphasizing others. I have even read some that claimed that only animal foods build our bodies; plant foods were described as just "cleansers". This might be true for cats, but in the context of human nutrition, it sounds like (intentionally?) disregarding the whole world of history and science.

I was a vegetarian from age 16 to 34, and for three of those years I was even a vegan. All that time I was in excellent health, which I mainly attribute to avoiding processed foods. Finally, good arguments and information I was not aware of before, convinced me that animals are an important part in ecological agriculture and that farming that includes animals causes much less suffering, erosion and other ecological damage than plants-only farming. Therefore, I now eat animal products, but I strictly limit myself to ecologically produced ones. To avoid industrial lies and loopholes (such as providing little patches for grazing for supposedly pasture-fed animals, but in reality those animals rarely go outside), I only buy from local farmers whom I know personally.

I was "converted" to vegetarianism by books I read, which sounded very scientific and reasonable, especially to my teenage self. However, considering how that information turned to be incomplete, I am now much more cautious about the authors' prejudices or corporate interests presented as seemingly sound science. I have read a huge amount of information regarding the recent "low carb, high protein" fad – and noticed that those books and articles are written very much like the ones that motivated me to become a vegetarian. It is almost like reading the same books, just adapted to another extreme. Here are the common elements I have noticed in *both* cases:

- claims about an "avant-garde" attitude and rejecting official,

176

corrupted science that "manipulated us all" (often a "righteously indignant" writing style)

- arguments related to prehistoric diet and lifestyle (interpreted to fit the author's theories or interests)

- selective examples of primitive tribes and their diets

- anecdotal approach and case studies (usually short-term ones). Such an approach is by itself problematic, because it does not represent general population.

- quoting scientific research (yet who knows how much of it was biased and incomplete, or how much were the conclusions twisted, taken out of context, or outright fabricated? There are many scientists around who are paid to do exactly that, and they do it very skillfully. Sometimes people who quote scientific studies twist and distort their conclusions.)

- ecology related arguments

- (selective) common sense

- positive feedback from happy followers and their stories of recovered health

- using fear (of disease and old age problems) and hope (promises of health)

- claims of rebellion against big corporations.

I believe that most of the benefits of both of those approaches come from rejecting processed and industrially grown food. Also, from reducing calories. Many people in our civilization are not aware that they simply eat TOO MUCH. We were often taught to eat more than we needed (as children) and we are constantly told that our bodies need a lot of protein, a lot of fiber, a lot of this vitamin or that mineral (some theories even recommend a lot of fat). Our bodies are biologically motivated to eat always a bit more than needed, to store for a possible future famine. Therefore, most of us eat more than we need, but believe we eat reasonable amounts. Then we search for culprits in different food categories and combinations.

Out of everything I have read, I now follow only the following diet principles:

- I avoid not only processed food, but also anything industrially grown (especially when it comes to animals, which are given hormones, drugs and food grown with toxic chemicals. Often that food is not what those animals would normally eat, but mostly GMO corn or soy)

- I eat small amounts of concentrated foods (high calorie content, small mass), and much more low-concentrated (low calorie, high in water)

- I take care to always eat slightly less than I think I need

- I find that diets that require a lot of calculating, measuring or (particularly) rejecting or eliminating certain food categories, are probably fads, based on biased and incomplete research.

Consequences

You will probably not be ruined if, from time to time, you eat something unhealthy – but you should take into serious consideration gradual, long-term consequences of your regular diet. Consider how your body will look or feel 15 to 20 years from now if you eat natural, fresh food, compared to continuing to eat like average people. You do not even have to speculate about the latter option – just look around and notice how average people, 15 to 20 years older than you, appear. Should you accept that as your unavoidable future at that age? I do not think so.

If you manage to avoid processed food for a couple of months, you will notice that you feel less interested in it and more aware that eating it would feel like eating plastics. Also, you will become more aware of the toxic effects that processed food has on your body: feelings of acidity, heaviness, lack of energy, perhaps even headaches or mild sickness. A body that is used to processed food, loses the ability to sense such warning signals.

For non-smokers, revulsion toward cigarette smoke, as well as to the very idea of inhaling that smoke, appears natural and obvious. Nonetheless, most non-smokers do something similar, by ingesting large quantities of industrial foods, which are incompatible with human health.

The emotional and physiological consequences of addictions to processed foods are usually milder than of addictions to alcohol, nicotine or drugs. This makes them more difficult to perceive and acknowledge.

Even people who know all these facts, often spontaneously use their defense mechanisms, by denying and/or minimizing their addicted behavior. These mechanisms are common for all addictions: fooling ourselves that we can easily give it up (starting next week!), that we have control, or that something that we want so much, that feels so good, cannot do us much harm.

The consumption of low quality food, lacking in vitamins, minerals and enzymes (artificial nutrients are a poor replacement!) results in malnutrition and deficiencies, even if one eats large quantities. This stimulates us to eat more frequently and have larger servings, without ever feeling well-fed in a healthy way. Calorie counting may decrease the amount of food consumed, but its nutritive value is not necessarily increased. As in other areas of life, the key is not in quantity but in quality. Many people who start to eat light, high quality food, become aware that now they need less food than before.

Other emotional aspects

Stephan von Stepski – Doliwa in his book "Theorie und Technik der analytischen Körpertherapie", says that, just as we can become addicted to food, we can also become addicted to strict diet rules. Thus, even the smallest deviation from those rules creates fear, guilt and other psychological and psychosomatic symptoms. Such people may perceive these symptoms as consequences of breaking the rules.

At the root of this problem is a need to control other aspects of life through food (a pattern also present in anorexia and bulimia). With this approach, people try to create an illusion of independence and well-being through their external behavior, instead of exploring their emotions and relationships.

If we carefully listen to our bodies, we will learn to recognize their subtle needs and warnings. However, it is important to learn the difference between healthy physical needs, and unhealthy, addictive, emotional needs. Many people who decide to listen to their bodies, use this idea as an excuse to follow their addictive needs and urges for pleasure, instead of the whole of their bodies.

I cannot easily define the differences between these two types of needs, since they are subtle bodily feelings. You can learn these differences through self-observation. One indication is that unhealthy needs are usually much stronger and more urgent, just as unhealthy emotions are often more overwhelming than healthy feelings.

Once you start following your body's signals, you will probably become more conscious of emotions that you were suppressing by food, or emotional needs that you were trying to fulfill through food. To fully resolve such problems, instead of just trying to control their consequences, you will likely need to work on the sources of those emotions. By doing so, you can reap great rewards, not only physical health, in fact your overall quality of life.

Practice

Whenever you crave a certain type of food (or anything addictive), observe your feelings. What emotional states do you hope to achieve? How could you create such feelings in ways other than eating?

Are you are trying to control or avoid some emotional states with food? Which ones? What other solutions can you find?

What happens after you eat the food you crave? Observe how you feel immediately afterwards, as well as after a few hours.

Have you experienced cravings for certain fresh fruits or vegetables? In what way were those feelings different from longings for processed foods?

Passionate and Magnificent Life

How did you react to this title? Did you gain or lose energy? Maybe, just for a moment, did you create a vision? Or, if you did not even try, did you feel burdened with fear of disappointment or a feeling of hopelessness?

Your life can be a magnificent adventure if you are not so discouraged by your thinking habits, that you cannot even imagine that better things are possible.

One of my favorite affirmations is "My life is magnificent and exciting". Imagine that you live the life of your dreams, enjoying high energy, beautiful relationships, appreciating your body and the world around you.

The responsibility is yours. I do not suggest that you could create such a life in a month or two. However, you will not create much if you give up easily and choose to complain rather than to solve challenges.

It is important to give yourself time and accept failure as a part of a natural learning process, as a way to gain wisdom and experience instead of as a proof of weakness – just like a child learning to walk may fall a thousand times, but keeps on trying.

Many people hope for dramatic life changes after resolving a trauma or limiting belief. It is pleasant to expect that everything will become easy and that our wishes will quickly come true. Often I hear (and I used to say it myself): "If I resolve this one thing, then I will be riding high!". However, unlike marketing promises, changes rarely happen automatically.

With every resolved belief, with every part of our identity that we integrate into our consciousness, we change – an increase in energy, motivation, self-esteem – and often it seems so natural that we might feel that it was always there. And indeed it was, except that we were hiding or sabotaging it. With each of those changes, we also increase our passion for life – a natural feeling of joy and gratitude for what life offers.

However, if you want real external results, you need to do more. You can start with cultivating that passion and learning to express it in the outside world. Do not sit and wait for the world to bring desired experiences to you. Join evening courses. Start meeting new people. Travel. Start a blog. Anything.

It is sad to see so many people living lives full of unpleasant feelings and low energy. They lack a true joy of life, which is much more than what is usually called passion. The feeling that I am trying to describe includes all of life, our whole identities as well as our entire surroundings: deep joy of pure existence, joy in being in our bodies, in every part of our lives, and a longing to share this experience.

For me, that feeling of passion often starts as a sense of uneasiness, a strange energy that is looking for a way out. In such moments, I sometimes feel an urge to distract myself with trivial activities. I believe that many people follow that urge, since this joy of life is strong, unusual and overwhelming. It feels like listening to my favorite music, but a hundred times stronger. Could it be that one reason we avoid our passion is that it might be difficult to accept our everyday, mundane lives and moods, if we allowed ourselves to feel passionate more often?

I usually feel this kind of passion in those periods when I intensely work on building self-love. Imagine how it would feel, if you were spending most of your time in such a state! – but we ignore it and cut it off just like many other suppressed emotions.

In my experience, resolving the causes of emotional problems – traumas and toxic beliefs – can bring unexpected benefits. Besides increased freedom and changed perspectives, you will create openness and space for new emotional states: beautiful feelings that you might have forgotten a long time ago – or never even experienced.

We might have a problem appreciating spontaneous good feelings, if we generally do not trust our emotions. In this case, we may only appreciate experiences acknowledged by external authorities, or feelings that arise while practicing someone else's methods.

There are many ways to evoke pleasant feelings that support personal development. However, if we do not deal with the hidden, painful parts of our subconscious, the effects of such methods will be temporary (which is still better than nothing). Once we heal and integrate rejected parts of ourselves, we provide room to naturally and spontaneously experience joy, love, passion and a state of integrity or wholeness.

Some of those new feelings will be subtle and unusual, while some might overwhelm you in unexpected moments, for example during everyday activities. If those new feelings are difficult to define and describe, you might well be in contact with parts of yourself that you hid or forgot before you learned to talk and think in words.

Many people, when they experience strong or unusual pleasant feelings, either ignore them or view them with suspicion. They may distract themselves (for example, some people feel an urge to smoke a cigarette after making love). I suggest the opposite: take time for those feelings, explore them, make them stronger and enjoy them! Treat them like you probably treat unpleasant feelings: contemplate them, express them, and talk about them to someone you trust. These feelings are luxuries, and it would be a pity not to enjoy them fully.

Many people have moments when they experience a sense of greatness; a feeling that they are born for something big, something beyond normal human existence. I believe that this might be true for all of us. A question is, will you actively engage yourself in realizing your potential, or will you wait for someone to do this for you?

APPENDIX: Exploring Emotions

This is an overview of a simple approach to exploring and befriending emotions, adapted to generic, average situations, using some simple elements from Soulwork Systemic Coaching. In this overview, I have excluded many unique elements and methods of the Soulwork approach, because they deal with complex patterns (e.g. transferences, identifications and complex conflicts), and require direct interactions with a trained coach.

It may not be easy to do this by yourself, since you need to switch your attention between rational self-guidance and emotional awareness. This approach is best applied to simple issues, or as support for in-depth sessions with a qualified Soulwork coach.

It is not always easy to distinguish simple from complex issues. Sometimes tiny "tics" expose difficult, deeply rooted patterns. I can only offer basic guidelines: practice with emotional issues that are only mildly unpleasant, with which you can remain adult and resourceful. Be aware that this is not a guarantee that you can do it all by yourself. Use caution and your common sense.

WARNING: As this process can bring strong emotions to consciousness, it is only appropriate for mentally healthy and stable people. Avoid trying to resolve strong emotions, if you do not feel emotionally stable, especially if you have been diagnosed with a mental disorder, or if you have recently used psychoactive substances or medications (including alcohol).

If you are going through a life crisis (such as loss of a family member, loss of a job, severe disease...) you might not be resourceful enough to explore your hidden emotions. Focus on resolving your immediate practical issues first.

If at any moment you feel that your emotions might overwhelm you and you may not be able to cope with them, immediately stop the exercise. This might indicate a need for professional help. This process is not a substitute for medical or psychiatric treatment. Do this only if you are willing to take full responsibility for any unpredicted consequences.

Do not try to guide other people through this process, unless you are professionally qualified to deal with such issues.

1) Define (as positively as you can) a goal you want to achieve, or choose an emotion you want to explore. Choose a realistic and ethical goal (not, for example, how to seduce as many people as possible).

2) If it is a goal, explore your feelings to find what stops you from achieving it, or at least what stops you from working on it. Which emotion(s) or physical sensation(s) appear?

3) Once you determine a limiting emotion, explore what ideas or beliefs it contains.

4) How old do you *emotionally* feel while in that state? Do you feel like a child, adult or an old person? If you feel that the emotion is childish, carry on.

(If an emotion feels like it belongs to an adult or an older person, it is possible that you are not aware of what is under the surface, or that this is an identification issue – that is, you have identified with someone (probably, but not necessarily, in your past).

Dissolving identifications is outside the scope of this book, but for more clarity, ask yourself: How long have I carried this emotion in my body? How old could I have been when I accepted it? Who or what does it remind me of?)

5) Imagine being a child of approximately that age, feeling that unpleasant emotion. Perhaps you will have insights about who or what the emotion is associated with.

6) What beliefs are associated with this emotion? Check for the most abstract, black and white, toxic beliefs about yourself, life or other people.

7) Ask yourself: How did I benefit by accepting such a belief? Why do I still carry it? (The benefits might not be obvious and logical to your adult self.)

8) If you have an insight about who may be associated with the emotion, imagine the perspectives of each of those important people. What motivated their behavior? What might they have hoped for? What might they have wanted from you?

9) What might those people have believed? How old were they *emotionally* in those moments? Who or what might you have reminded them of?

186

10) Communicate with your inner child from your position as an adult. (It might help if you imagine that your inner child is sitting on another chair). Assume that this part of you does not know you have grown up. Imagine talking about anything that you feel your inner child needs to know. Perhaps remember some of the most beautiful and inspiring moments of your life and give those memories to your inner child. Remind the child how much time has passed and how old you are now.

11) Ask yourself, what part(s) of yourself you had to hide or forget, to create or accept your toxic beliefs (the ones from step 6). This is usually a healthy quality – self-esteem, joy, playfulness –that is quite opposite to the toxic belief. Try to remember or imagine how you felt *before* that unpleasant experience, before you split off that part of you. Relive this healthy feeling as strongly as possible.

14) Now observe the unpleasant experience with your new perspective and insight. How does that experience change with your healthier emotional perception?

15) Imagine how your childhood, adolescent life, adult years … would be different if you had not created or accepted that toxic belief, if you have never split off that healthy part of yourself.

16) How would you change the way you presently live your life, if you express this healthy part of yourself?

17) To continue your integration, in the next few days (and weeks) spend as much time as possible in this healthy state and choose your behaviors from that state.

Acknowledgments:

I have built my knowledge and experience on the efforts and trust of many people.

I have learned a huge amount about human systems and emotional patterns from Martyn Carruthers. His method (Soulwork Systemic Coaching) is a big part of the theoretical and practical background of this book. It gave me many useful tools for helping my clients and exploring their realities. Martyn also invited me to teach with him in several countries, which were precious experiences. He invested many hours in tidying up the English version of the book, making it more readable for English-speaking public, suggesting changes and encouraging humor in it. He is continuously in my life with his encouragement and love.

Simon Stella from Caledon, Canada, did the final proof-reading of the English version, fueled by friendliness and love. He put a lot of attention and thought into every single page. Thanks Simon!

I want to thank our organizers around the world for the opportunity for me to gain experience by teaching in their countries. Amongst them are: Leon Deith in Britain, Shannon Hand in Canada, Joanna Mądrzak in Poland, Samuel Grznár in Slovakia, Jivan Leela in Czech Republic and Ivonne Delaflor-Alexander in Mexico.

Sanja Tatalovic, the editor of the Croatian edition of this book, first recognized the potential of my articles and suggested putting them together into a book. She put a lot of energy and enthusiasm into editing the first version of this book.

Mirjam Kolenc-Ercegovac gives continuous enthusiasm and encouragement. Sometimes I think she is even more excited and delighted with my successes than I am!

I have learned from countless authors who deserve to be credited for the existence of this book. Some of them are: Alice Miller, Harville Hendrix, John Bradshaw, John Gray, Stephan von Stepski – Doliwa ... You can find more in the chapter, "Recommended Reading". I have necessarily only included a small number of the books that I have read and appreciated there.

A final thanks to hundreds of my clients and readers who trusted me, shared their stories with me and encouraged me with their enthusiastic feedback. I cannot name them here, but I still want to express my gratitude.

Recommended Reading

Martyn Carruthers: articles on www.soulwork.net website

Harville Hendrix: *"Getting the Love You Want: A Guide for Couples"*, St. Martin's Press, 1988 ; *"Keeping the Love You Find"*, Atria, 1993

Stephan von Stepski – Doliwa: *"Theorie und Technik der analytischen Körpertherapie"*, Peter Lang, 1989

John Bradshaw: *"Family Secrets"*, Bantam Books, 1995; *"Bradshaw On: Healing the Shame that Binds You"*, Deerfield Beach, Florida: Health Communications, 1988

Steve Biddulph: *"The Secret of Happy Children"*, Da Capo Press; 2002

John Gray: *"Men Are from Mars, Women Are from Venus"*, HarperCollins, 1992

Alice Miller: *"The Drama of the Gifted Child"*, Basic Books, 1997; *"For Your Own Good"*, Farrar, Straus and Giroux, 1990

Harvey Karp: *"The Happiest Toddler on the Block"*, Bantam, 2008

Marie Pipher: *"Reviving Ophelia: Saving the Selves of Adolescent Girls"*, Riverhead Trade, 2005

Barbara Goulter, Joan Minninger: *"The Father - Daughter Dance"*, Avon Books, 1994

Carl Rogers: *"On Becoming a Person"*, Constable, 2004

Diane Chelsom Gossen: *"Restitution: Restructuring School Discipline"*, New View Pubns, 1996

Adele Faber and Elaine Mazlish : *"How to Talk so Kids Will Listen"*, Nightingale-Conant, 2002

Sean Neill: *"Classroom nonverbal communication"*, Routledge, 1991

Jerry D. Twentier : *"The Positive Power of Praising People"*, McGraw-Hill, 1998

Jerry Mander: *"Four Arguments for the Elimination of Television"*, William Morrow Paperbacks, 1978

Barbara De Angelis: *"Real moments"*, Dell, 1995

Michael Pollan: *"In Defense of Food"*, Penguin Books, 2009

Jeffrey M. Masson and Susan McCarthy: *"When Elephants Weep: The Emotional Lives of Animals"*, Delta, 1996

Emotional Maturity in Everyday Life
Copyright: Kosjenka Muk
Published: 30th March 2013

ISBN: 978-953-95788-2-2

Originaly published in Croatia as "Emocionalna zrelost u svakodnevnom zivotu"

CPSIA information can be obtained at www.ICGtesting.com
Printed in the USA
LVOW05s2128181213

365927LV00029B/1221/P

9 789539 578822